1,000,000 Books

are available to read at

www.ForgottenBooks.com

Read online
Download PDF
Purchase in print

ISBN 978-1-331-89706-4
PIBN 10251198

This book is a reproduction of an important historical work. Forgotten Books uses state-of-the-art technology to digitally reconstruct the work, preserving the original format whilst repairing imperfections present in the aged copy. In rare cases, an imperfection in the original, such as a blemish or missing page, may be replicated in our edition. We do, however, repair the vast majority of imperfections successfully; any imperfections that remain are intentionally left to preserve the state of such historical works.

Forgotten Books is a registered trademark of FB &c Ltd.
Copyright © 2018 FB &c Ltd.
FB &c Ltd, Dalton House, 60 Windsor Avenue, London, SW19 2RR.
Company number 08720141. Registered in England and Wales.

For support please visit www.forgottenbooks.com

1 MONTH OF FREE READING

at

www.ForgottenBooks.com

By purchasing this book you are eligible for one month membership to ForgottenBooks.com, giving you unlimited access to our entire collection of over 1,000,000 titles via our web site and mobile apps.

To claim your free month visit:

www.forgottenbooks.com/free251198

* Offer is valid for 45 days from date of purchase. Terms and conditions apply.

English
Français
Deutsche
Italiano
Español
Português

www.forgottenbooks.com

Mythology Photography **Fiction**
Fishing Christianity **Art** Cooking
Essays Buddhism Freemasonry
Medicine **Biology** Music **Ancient Egypt** Evolution Carpentry Physics
Dance Geology **Mathematics** Fitness
Shakespeare **Folklore** Yoga Marketing
Confidence Immortality Biographies
Poetry **Psychology** Witchcraft
Electronics Chemistry History **Law**
Accounting **Philosophy** Anthropology
Alchemy Drama Quantum Mechanics
Atheism Sexual Health **Ancient History**
Entrepreneurship Languages Sport
Paleontology Needlework Islam
Metaphysics Investment Archaeology
Parenting Statistics Criminology
Motivational

BY THE SAME AUTHOR

IN COLLABORATION WITH

GEORGE HUBBARD, F.S.A.
VICE-PRESIDENT OF THE ROYAL INSTITUTE
OF BRITISH ARCHITECTS

NEOLITHIC DEW-PONDS AND CATTLE-WAYS

With 29 Illustrations

FIRST EDITION, 1905

SECOND EDITION, 1907

Royal 4to, 4s. 6d. net.

LONGMANS, GREEN AND CO.
LONDON, NEW YORK, BOMBAY, AND CALCUTTA

THE
FATE OF EMPIRES

BEING AN INQUIRY INTO THE STABILITY OF CIVILISATION

BY

ARTHUR JOHN HUBBARD

M.D. (Dunelm.)

LONGMANS, GREEN AND CO.
39 PATERNOSTER ROW, LONDON
NEW YORK, BOMBAY, AND CALCUTTA
1913

All rights reserved

DEDICATED

TO

MY WIFE

FOR

A THOUSAND GOOD REASONS

A. J. H.

288390

PREFACE

The turning-point in past civilisations has been marked, again and again, by the appearance of Socialism coincidently with a failure of the birth-rate. During the lifetime of the present generation these two phenomena have assumed a more and more prominent position among the races of white men, and it has been my object to show how critical the position of any civilisation is when it reaches the point at which they are simultaneously manifested. I have tried to demonstrate that they are caused by the same force acting upon different materials, and that the supersession of that force by another and more powerful is indispensable to the stability of civilisation. My theme is not one that has permitted me to write with a running pen.

My most sincere thanks are due to Mrs. Renney Allinson for an immensity of kind and efficient help. She has not only prepared my manuscript for the press and compiled the index, but has rendered me valuable assistance by criticism and reference to authors.

I heartily thank, too, Mr. Clement John Wilkinson, M.R.C.S.Eng., alike for the welcome encouragement that he has given me during the progress of my task, and for the valuable time and work that he devoted to it.

The reader will see that this essay could not have been written had it not been preceded by Mr. Benjamin Kidd's great work, *Social Evolution*.

A. J. H.

Little Dean, Newnham-on-Severn,
    Gloucestershire,
        October 1912.

SYNOPSIS OF CONTENTS

PART I

THE BASIS OF A PERMANENT CIVILISATION

CHAPTER I

THE ANTECEDENTS OF CIVILISATION

	PAGE
Is a permanent civilisation a possibility?	4
Necessary to discover the forces that make for growth, and those that make for decay of civilisation?	4
These forces are constants	5
History only gives the resultant of these forces; therefore the forces themselves are not discoverable in history. Analogy of the parallelogram of forces in mechanics	6
These forces can be identified when the whole history of organic advance is reviewed	6
Organic advance is intermittent: a new "method" is adopted at each stage	8
List of these "methods"	9
Definition of word "Instinct" when used in succeeding pages .	10
Definition of word "Reason" when used in succeeding pages .	10

CHAPTER II

THE METHOD OF INSTINCT

The standing problem in any method is that of reconciling the Individual (who dies) with the Race (which persists) . .	13
The method of Instinct solves the problem by means of inborn impulse	13
Inborn impulse is an appurtenance of the Race, and merely sacrifices the Individual	14
Therefore it involves unlimited waste of individual lives . .	17
This wastefulness is necessarily inherent in the method . .	18

	PAGE
Therefore the method itself is imperfect	18
Fauna of previous geologic epochs probably purely instinctive	21
Modern animals not descended from types most prominent in past geological epochs	21
Modern animals possess a modicum of Reason	22
Which lessened the wastefulness of pure Instinct and enabled their progenitors to displace a purely instinctive fauna.	24
Thus Instinct is superseded by Reason	24
But Reason, in its turn, will be under the necessity of solving the same standing problem, viz. the problem of reconciling the transitory Individual with the long life of the Race	25

CHAPTER III

THE METHOD OF REASON

In man Reason has become the overlord of Instinct, and effects an immense saving of waste. Man owes his position at the head of the organic world to the energy thus set free, but his dependence on the method of Reason is absolute	27 and 28
Reason is an appurtenance of the Individual, not of the Race	29
Under Reason, interest takes the place that was occupied by impulse under Instinct. An attenuation of the stress of life results	29
The general stress of life is resolvable into two:	
A. The rivalry among contemporaries: the stress of competition	31
B. The effort involved in the nurture and care of children: the stress of reproduction	31
Necessary to examine the manner in which Reason deals with each of these stresses separately	32
Definition of the words "Society" and "Race" as used in succeeding pages	33
Conception indicated by word "Society" is purely the creation of Reason	33
Examination of interaction of interest of individual with that of Society resolves itself into an examination of the stress of competition	34
While examination of interaction of the interest of the Individual with that of the Race resolves itself into an examination of the stress of reproduction	34
Reason being an appurtenance of the Individual, we have to ask whither his interest leads him in dealing with each of these stresses	34

SYNOPSIS OF CONTENTS

CHAPTER IV

REASON IN RELATION TO COMPETITION: THE INTEREST OF THE INDIVIDUAL IN RELATION TO SOCIETY

	PAGE
No disparity in point of duration in time between Individual and Society: therefore not antecedently impossible that their interests may be reconciled	36
"Is it to the interest of the Individual to abolish competition?"	38
The proposal to abolish competition excites a sense of revulsion, and the arguments against it are inspired by that sentiment rather than purely rational	38
Thus it has been urged that slavery to a bureaucracy would result. But that slavery would be less than the slavery to competitive conditions of life	40
Again, it has been urged that degeneration of "character" would ensue. But all that is required is a rational character	41
The revulsion of feeling, and the arguments founded upon it, are not rational	42
Relief from the incubus of competition is to the interest of Society	42
"Is it in the power of the Individual to abolish competition?"	42
It has been urged that the instinctive impulse leading to individual ownership renders its abolition impossible	43
But that argument ignores the ever-increasing ascendancy of Reason over Instinct	45
Office of Reason is to prevent the wastefulness of the competitive method of Instinct: Socialism the inevitable outcome of the working of pure Reason. Pure Reason can reconcile the interest of the Individual with that of Society	46

CHAPTER V

REASON IN RELATION TO REPRODUCTION: THE INTEREST OF THE INDIVIDUAL IN RELATION TO THE RACE

Reason takes no account of the interest of the Race: only of the interest of the Individual	48
"Is it to the interest of the Individual to decline the provision of future generations?"	49

THE FATE OF EMPIRES

	PAGE
It may be said that the question is unfair because Instinct intervenes, and Reason does not stand alone	49
But, again, that argument ignores the ever-increasing ascendancy of Reason over Instinct	49
Life an entailed estate. That the owner should be constrained to leave it undiminished is of the essence of the entail. Reason supplies no constraint, and it is to the interest of the life-tenant to break the entail	51
"Is it in his power to break the entail?"	52
Ask the Registrar-General	53
Pure Reason cannot reconcile the interests of the Individual with that of the Race	54

CHAPTER VI

RELATIVE INTERESTS OF SOCIETY AND THE RACE

The triangle of interests	55
As reproductive activity is lessened, the stress of competition becomes less severe. Converse also true	56
But Reason does not ask that the stresses should be lessened, but abolished	57
The interest of Society is as hostile to the Race as is that of the Individual	59

CHAPTER VII

CONDEMNATION OF THE METHOD OF REASON

The revolt against the social stress occurs synchronously with the revolt against the racial stress, and marks a definite point of growth of Reason relatively to Instinct	61
The power of controlling the birthrate is a new evolutionary environment, purely the creation of Reason	62
This environment is deadly to the Race: example of France	64
Permanence of a civilisation that is founded on pure Reason is a flat impossibility	64

CHAPTER VIII

THE METHOD OF RELIGIOUS MOTIVE

Therefore a supra-rational method requires investigation	67
To take precedence of Reason such a method must be free from the cause of disability that is common to its predecessors,	

SYNOPSIS OF CONTENTS

	PAGE
and more particularly from the form of disability that is special to Reason	68
What is the cause of the disability that is common to its predecessors?	68
Not one has failed to make good the deficiency in its predecessor; but each extension of environment being still geocentric, has raised fresh difficulties	70
Therefore the method of Religious Motive can only be successful if it provides an environment that does not admit of extension	70
Taking cognisance of the infinite it fulfils this requirement	71
The form of disability that is special to Reason is failure to provide a basis for disinterested conduct	71
But, when in relation with the infinite, the significance of life is in service, and duty takes the place of interest	72
Definition of the word "Religion" as used in succeeding pages	72

CHAPTER IX

THE RELATION OF THE METHOD OF RELIGIOUS MOTIVE TO THE SOCIAL STRESS: THE DUTY OF THE INDIVIDUAL WITH REGARD TO SOCIETY

The lifelong self-sacrifice of a rational being cannot be justified on geocentric grounds. But the supra-rational method is another fresh departure, dependent on the reality of the cosmocentric significance of conduct	74
That significance in its turn dependent on freedom of the will. If that freedom is in our possession, then conduct is invested with the dignity of cosmocentric significance	76
"Is it the duty of the Individual to accept a competitive life?"	77
No: as in the method of Instinct, unlimited competition is socially immoral	77
"Is it his duty to accept a non-competitive life?"	78
No: for the non-competitive life of the method of Reason is socially a-moral	80
Thus a deadlock occurs, and the question arises: "Is it in any way in the power of the Individual so to frame his life that his social conduct shall be of cosmocentric significance?"	81
Two elements are necessary to significance of conduct: liberty and law	81

	PAGE
Competitive method furnishes liberty and a non-competitive method furnishes law. If each were taken as the complement of the other the deadlock would be removed.	82
But each method excludes the other	83
Therefore the question arises: "Does the Individual possess a solvent of each that enables them to enter into combination?"	83
Yes: Religious Motive has claims to allegiance that are superior to either	84
In the absence of this solvent the purely rational being is bound to his method, but in its presence he is not.	84
He has power of selection from each of the lower methods: he can retain the liberty of the one and the law of the other	85
The cosmocentric method thus provides a machinery that is perfect for significant social conduct	86

CHAPTER X

RELATION OF THE METHOD OF RELIGIOUS MOTIVE TO THE RACIAL STRESS: THE DUTY OF THE INDIVIDUAL WITH REGARD TO THE RACE

"Is it the duty of the Individual to carry the multiplication of the Race to its utmost limits, as in the method of Instinct, or to act in a contrary manner, as in the method of Reason?"	87
The method of Instinct is racially a-moral	88
The method of Reason is racially immoral	89
Thus a deadlock occurs analogous to that reached in the last chapter, and the question arises: "Is it in the power of the Individual to avoid, at the same time, the racial a-morality of the one and the racial immorality of the other?"	89
Diagram of geocentric systems as they appear from the point of view of Religious Motive	90
With the method of Reason comes racial liberty, and with the method of Instinct racial law. Significance in racial conduct only attained by their amalgamation. This cannot occur spontaneously	91
But can occur in the presence of the external authority of Religious Motive, which thus provides a machinery that is perfect for significant racial conduct	92

SYNOPSIS OF CONTENTS

CHAPTER XI

MUTUAL RELATIONS OF SOCIETY AND THE RACE UNDER THE METHOD OF RELIGIOUS MOTIVE

	PAGE
The future of the Race is far removed from the outlook of the Individual on account of their disparity in length of life	95
Thus it becomes the office of Society, acting under the method of Religious Motive, to provide the means whereby racial duty, already recognised, can be carried out—to provide, that is, a nexus that shall join together the Individual and the Race	96
This link provided in the social institution of the family	96
Hence the semi-religious veneration for the family	97
The family as an institution cannot be justified in pure Reason	98
Legislative attacks on the family react on the Race	98
The honour in which the family is held as an institution gives the measure of the vitality of a given civilisation	99

CHAPTER XII

JUSTIFICATION OF THE METHOD OF RELIGIOUS MOTIVE

This method not yet the dominating influence in the civilisation of the white man	100
Its failure not to be attributed to the method, but to the fact that the method has not been adopted	101
Under the method of Religious Motive, social conduct is that of a trustee and racial conduct that of the life-tenant of an entailed estate	101
Quotation from Gospel according to the Egyptians	102
The co-ordination of law and liberty is the very note of the method of Religious Motive, but many have sought and none found it within the confines of Reason	102
Reason seeks but cannot attain a permanent civilisation. Its attainment is only possible as an entirely unessential property of the method of Religious Motive	103

PART II

HISTORICAL ILLUSTRATION OF THE PRINCIPLES INDICATED IN THE PRECEDING CHAPTERS

CHAPTER I

ROME AND CHINA

PAGE

As already pointed out in Part I, Chap. I, the forces that make for the growth or the decay of a civilisation cannot be divined from history. But when these forces have been identified already, it is quite possible to trace their working in history, and, moreover, it is necessary to do so in order to test the truth of the general principles laid down in Part I . 107
For this purpose we shall choose two great civilisations that were in existence about the beginning of the Christian Era: the Roman and the Chinese. The one disappeared, but the other remains, and is still the most tremendous factor in the world of to-day 109

CHAPTER II

RELIGION UNDER THE ROMAN EMPIRE

Do we find ourselves in the presence of religious systems that formed part of the polity of the State, or of systems that were cosmocentric? 114
Evidence that they were geocentric 115
With two exceptions, viz. Judaism and Christianity. These two were intolerable to the geocentric Roman Empire . . 117
Treatment accorded to Judaism and Christianity . . . 118
The Roman Empire shows the triumph of Reason. Therefore we must expect to see the exaltation of Society and the decay of the Race 122

SYNOPSIS OF CONTENTS xvii

CHAPTER III

SOCIETY UNDER THE ROMAN EMPIRE

PAGE

The emperors. To the modern mind many of them seem pathological 124
But they were not unpopular 125
They were merely typical of their age 125
The Municipalities. They were highly organised, and largely supplanted the family 126
Literature. Rudimentary character of the ideals of goodness set up by the moralists. Descriptions of Roman Society given by the satirists are not preposterous 127
Trade Unions and Socialism. Efforts to avoid stress of competition 128
These efforts culminate in the vast socialistic decree of Diocletian 132
The splendour of Society under the Roman Empire . . . 133

CHAPTER IV

THE FAMILY AND THE RACE UNDER THE ROMAN EMPIRE

Forms of the monogamous family: Cognation and agnation. The family in early Roman history and throughout Chinese history is agnatic 134
Cognation shows us the family in its contact with Society; agnation shows it in contact with the Race 136
Marriage in Rome: confarreation, coemption, usus. Divorce: general aversion from matrimony in any form . . . 137
Infanticide: abortion. Advantages of childlessness. "A man who married was regarded as hardly in his senses" . . 140
Augustus sets himself to save the Race: methods adopted by him: the Lex Julia: its three parts: it attempts to make marriage and the possession of a family fashionable 141
The Lex Pappia Poppæa, an extension of the Lex Julia . . 142
Is not allowed to become a dead letter 143
These laws do not have even a temporary success . . . 143
Augustus and the Equites 144
The numbers of the State are therefore kept up by manumission of persons of servile birth. But the success of this measure is only temporary 145

xviii   THE FATE OF EMPIRES

PAGE

Constantine removes the seat of imperial power from Rome to Constantinople, and a contemporary writer, Lactantius, refers to the ominous depopulation of Italy 147

CHAPTER V

GREECE

Eminence of Reason in ancient Greece 148
Brevity of the duration of this eminence 148
Rapidity of the extermination of this Greek Race is in direct ratio to its pre-eminence in Reason 149
Suggestion that eugenic measures led to this sudden appearance of pre-eminence in Reason. Quotation from Dr. Bateson's work on Mendelism 150
The basis of a stable civilisation is not to be found in eugenics . 151

CHAPTER VI

RELIGION IN CHINA

Chinese religious conditions are the opposite of those obtaining in Western civilisations. 152
Tao-ism. The meaning that it has for the Chinese people. The writer's experience in a temple in China 153
Tao-ism is not geocentric. It does not inculcate obedience to the State. It ignores the interest of Society . . . 156
Therefore, in the ordering of social conduct, the Chinese have had to fall back upon the teachings of Confucius, an ethical philosopher 156
We may look for results exactly opposite to those seen in the Roman Empire 157

CHAPTER VII

SOCIETY IN CHINA

Chinese associations of labourers are not formed to restrict competition 158
The severity of the social stress is unmitigated, and social conditions are squalid 160
Nevertheless there is high development of Reason . . . 166

SYNOPSIS OF CONTENTS xix

CHAPTER VIII

THE FAMILY AND THE RACE IN CHINA

PAGE

The agnatic family is the supreme institution, and all other institutions are contributory to it 169
Thus the Race is maintained, but, owing to neglect of social duty, only in spite of immense difficulties 169
These difficulties are :
    I. Impotence and maladministration of the State. This leads to recurrent civil wars and disturbances, accompanied by enormous loss of life 170
    Also to loss of life from famine 171
    2. Neglect of science. This leads to an appalling rate of infant mortality 172
Exposure of female infants is not to be confounded with the infanticide that prevailed in the Roman Empire . . . 173
Neglect of science also leads to loss of life from preventable disease 174
Malaria not less present in China than in ancient Greece and Rome 174
Nevertheless all these drawbacks count for little when opposed to the power of an unrestricted birthrate 174
That power has continuously preserved the Chinese Race and civilisation from the most remote antiquity, and their future is incalculable 175
Note on the Jewish Race, and on ancient Egypt 175

CHAPTER IX

THE INDISPENSABLE BASIS OF A STABLE CIVILISATION

China furnishes an incomplete example of the method of Religious Motive, because it shows only the transformation of the service of the Race into the means of performing cosmocentric duty, and fails to show any similar transformation of the complementary service of Society. . The method of Religious Motive, in its entirety, would show us the reconciliation of the service of the one with the service of the other by the

transformation of the service of both into the means of performing cosmocentric duty 177
Whether or no a true and stable civilisation can be realised depends upon whether or no Reason provides a valid ground for this transformation. Position of the theologian. 178
The paradox of the method of Religious Motive . . . 179

INDEX 181

PART I

THE BASIS OF A PERMANENT CIVILISATION

THE FATE OF EMPIRES

CHAPTER I

THE ANTECEDENTS OF CIVILISATION

THE question of the fate of the existing civilisation of Europe and America gives rise to one of the most interesting speculations that can occupy the mind, and the white man of to-day possesses the records of so many civilisations that have proved unstable, that the past spreads before him, for his learning, the vision of which Keble wrote, and he sees:

> "The giant forms of empires on their way
> To ruin: one by one,
> They tower and they are gone."

If he is oppressed by the repetitions of history, he may exclaim, with the melancholy emperor, Marcus Aurelius, that "All things move in a circle." Or, perhaps in a braver mood, he may say that progress is intermittent, alternately falling back and anon coming forward at a higher level. He may believe that our present civilisation is indeed better than those that have collapsed, but he fears that its glory also will pass away, to be followed, in its turn—in some remote extension of the future—by a higher order. Or, again, he may hope that, in spite of many analogies with those that have preceded it, our civilisation will not be lost, will not become merely a few ruins and a legend, but that its indefinite growth will prove it to be a permanent possession of the human race.

The question, by its very nature, does not allow of mathematical statement, nor will the scientific methods applicable to chemistry or physics avail. For we shall deal with the works of the human mind, and with human affairs, in a region wherein we shall see that the immediate decay or the endless growth of our civilisation is not subject to a fixed law, but depends, from generation to generation, upon the course of action that is taken.

All that can be ascertained, even by the most successful investigation, is a distinction between the constructive and the destructive forces; the discovery of the underlying principle that has promoted the growth of the civilisations and empires of the past, and the determination of the cause of their decay. If we can do this successfully, we shall possess nothing less than the knowledge of good and evil in the State, and we shall be provided with an understanding of the conditions that decide between the future loss of the civilisation that is our heritage, and its unlimited expansion.

Such a knowledge is not to be superficially acquired. When, for instance, we are told that the decline of Rome was caused by the luxury and effeminacy of the Romans, we are told exactly

ANTECEDENTS OF CIVILISATION

nothing. We require to know how and why such a change came over the noble spirit of the Romans of an earlier day. Furthermore, we require to know the cause of the strange spectacle of a similar occurrence in all the great Western civilisations of the past—in Babylon, Thebes, and Athens, as well as in Rome.

The cause of such a change can only be found in the fact that, in the decaying State, the force that had previously made for growth was overmatched by that which made for dissolution. It is important to observe that the phenomena which attend this change are invariable, although they appear under the most dissimilar circumstances, and in ages widely removed from one another. The forces themselves, then, must be constants, and we must seek for their origin far below and away from the surface of recorded history. History, in fact, like the world around us, gives only the resultant of these forces. An illustration may be found in the proposition that is known in mechanics as that of the "parallelogram of forces." In this, two forces meet at an angle, and lines are drawn to represent them. The direction of the lines gives the direction of the forces, and the lines are drawn of a proper length to represent the magnitude of the forces relatively to one another. A parallelogram is constructed upon these lines, and a diagonal is drawn from their point of meeting to the opposite corner of the parallelogram. This diagonal will represent the resultant of the two forces under consideration, both in direction and magnitude.

Recorded history, so far as our present purpose is concerned, gives only this resultant of two component forces, one of these being that which makes for growth, and the other that which makes for decay. Of the work of these two forces, apart from the resultant, there neither is, nor can be, any record. A further analogy, that is of the greatest consequence, must be pointed out. As in mechanics, so in history, from the resultant it is impossible to divine either the direction or the magnitude of the components, for the possible ratios of direction and magnitude that would produce a given resultant are innumerable.

If, therefore, we would trace their operation in history, we must first find the components themselves. Then, indeed, if our search is successful, such a discovery will enable us to apportion to each of them separately the part that it contributes to the complex that we have before us.

The forces that we seek, or their more or less analogous predecessors, must be ultimately descended from forces that have been in operation from the very beginning. We must, then, commence our search, not where the conditions are so intricate as to make it hopeless—not, that is, even among the records of the most humble civilisation—but far away amid the more simple methods of animal life. For history itself reports only the end of a vast journey. The journey begins with the lowly beginnings of organic life, and is continued in successive marches; but it is the arrival alone that concerns the historian.

When we survey the journey as a whole, we

ANTECEDENTS OF CIVILISATION 7

recognise the broad fact of advance and growth. Nevertheless it is interrupted occasionally by retreat and decay, as, for example, in the case of the extinction of the monstrous fauna of the

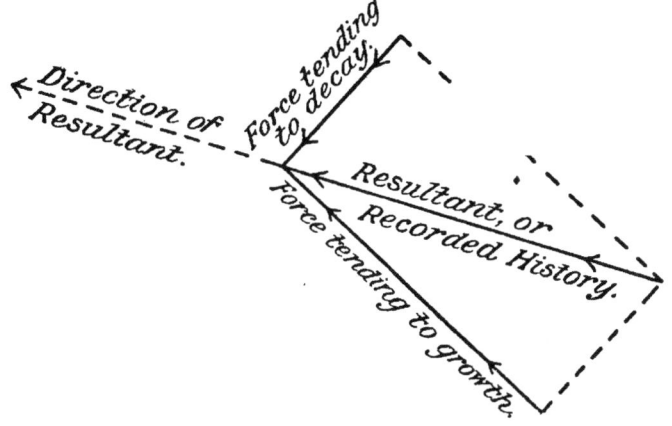

CONDITIONS OF GROWTH.

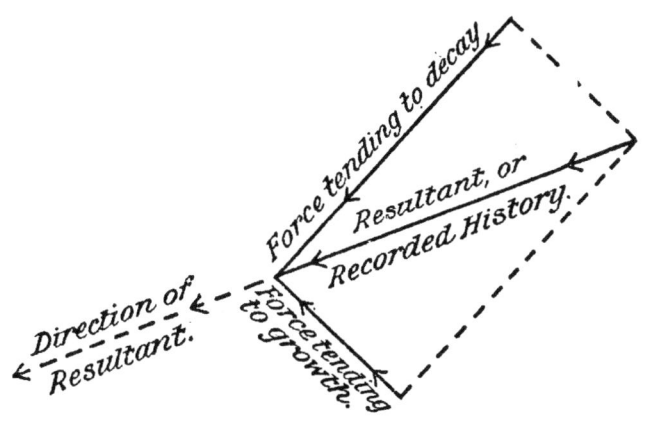

CONDITIONS OF DECAY.

Miocene period. Modern forms of life are not directly descended from the forms that were then most prominent; another route was taken, and so the advance continued. Such periods of decay show that the journey has been accomplished in a series of stages, by one method after another, and not continuously. In this respect the manner of organic progress shows a curiously close resemblance to the course of human invention. It is a matter of common observation that, when any human contrivance has been brought to a high stage of practical usefulness, further improvement on the same lines becomes extremely difficult. A state of high perfection is reached under the given conditions, and then a further advance is attained, not by improvements in the existing mechanism, but by a fresh start under new conditions. Thus, the sailing ship and the old system of coaching, when they were superseded by steam locomotion, were as nearly perfect as their circumstances permitted. The steam locomotive seems now to admit of little further improvement, and we are witnessing its supersession by electric traction and the internal-combustion engine.

So also is it in the history of organic advance: every stage will be found to be governed, not primarily by a change of form, but by the dominance of a new method or idea, whereby life can be maintained on a higher scale; and changes of form, as in the case of human invention, are but secondary. The outstanding point is, that each stage in such a history of invention is dominated by an entirely fresh method, and that the new mechanism is but the expression thereof.

Again, it will be found that none of the more important of the old methods is discarded; but that the new methods, one by one, are superimposed each upon its predecessor. The horse still works for us, although the steam locomotive is already passing into a less prominent position, and it is still necessary for us to use our feet, although the horse has been at our service for unnumbered ages.

In like wise, it is evident that the primitive methods of organic existence are not discarded, but that the new method is superimposed upon the old. Thus considered, the successive steps or methods of maintaining life during the advance from the protozoal organism to man may be shown as follows:—

1. Reflex Action.
2. Reflex Action *plus* Instinct.
3. Reflex Action *plus* Instinct *plus* Reason.
4. Reflex Action *plus* Instinct *plus* Reason *plus* Religious Motive.

Here Reflex Action, the power of involuntary response to an entirely external stimulus, is the first and most primitive step. The value of such power of response to some simple but frequently-repeated external occurrence is obvious. It is by the development of Reflex Action that the limpet contrives to maintain life upon a wave-swept rock. The waves break upon it, and, in response to the blows, it must cling intermittently to the rock. Thus life has succeeded in the occupation of a more extended area, an area wherein the possession of reflex power is not merely useful, but is essential.

Nevertheless, that area is strictly limited. In the first place, the power is only called into action by a stimulus external to the reflex mechanism itself. Herein is to be found the disability of merely reflex power, as contrasted with Instinct—as contrasted, that is, with the possession of useful inborn impulses.

In the second place, the reflex mechanism, under the pressure of its accustomed stimulus, acts inevitably even though the action may be self-destructive. Thus, for instance, the respiratory centre is called into action by a stimulus that, in its case, is a deficiency of oxygen in the blood. The *besoin de respirer* is imperative whether the air inspired be pure or impure—carbonic acid or atmospheric air. Granted the stimulus, there is no choice: so far as the reflex mechanism is concerned, it is helplessly at the mercy of its immediate surroundings. In respect to this second disability Instinct, the succeeding stage, stands in no contrast to reflex power. The inborn impulses of Instinct are obeyed just as blindly as the external stimuli that lead to reflex movement. Thus, for example, the tragic migrations of the Scandinavian lemming sometimes end at last by drowning in an attempt to cross the sea: the roaming impulse may be, in a majority of their migrations, most useful, but it is followed as unswervingly as though it were a reflex action. Pure Instinct, knowing nothing beyond the immediate gratification of the inborn impulse, is at the mercy of its immediate surroundings no less than Reflex Action. Thus reflex power and Instinct share the second disability in common, and it is not until we reach the development of Reason—the power of drawing inferences —that we find it made good by the conscious and deliberate pursuit of interest. In due course Reason will be found to be marred by a disability peculiar to itself—a disability that, in its turn, is only to be made good by the adoption of yet another line of advance.

CHAPTER II

THE METHOD OF INSTINCT

THE higher plane of existence that becomes possible with the appearance of the method of the inborn impulses of Instinct is most interesting. But before we proceed it will be well to be definite as to the connotation of the words " pure Instinct," or, more briefly, " Instinct," when they are used in these pages. By them we shall mean the possession of inherited inborn impulse, and the absence of any tincture of Reason—any tincture, that is, of the power of drawing inferences.

Our interest is excited by the fact that, when we have seen not only the advantages of Instinct, but also the limitations of its usefulness, then we shall perceive the exact manner in which the succeeding stage of Reason came to be of value.

We have already compared these stages to the steps of human invention in overcoming the difficulties of locomotion; and now the analogy may be carried yet further. The methods of dealing with this difficulty vary from age to age, becoming, age by age, more and more efficient. Nevertheless, the difficulty itself—the difficulty of locomotion—ever remains the same problem. It is only the solutions that are progressive, and succeed one to another.

So it is with the stages of organic advance.

THE METHOD OF INSTINCT 13

The methods vary whereby life is maintained on higher and higher planes, but the problem wherewith these methods deal does not itself undergo any change. What, then, is this underlying and invariable difficulty?

The life of the individual organism, as we know it, is a transitory possession: the life of the species or Race is age-long, and the life of the permanent Race is dependent upon the acts of the transitory Individual. The standing problem is to bring about the reconciliation of these two—in effect, it is to bring to bear upon the Individual such influences as shall lead him to secure for the Race a future in which he has no part or lot.

This is the riddle of the Sphinx to which a satisfactory answer must be returned under pain of racial death. At every stage—under Reflex Power, under Instinct, under Reason, under Religious Motive—and at all times, a more or less efficient *modus vivendi* between the transitory and the permanent must be provided, for extinction is the penalty of failure to do so.

By what method, then, has this problem been answered by Instinct? What are the advantages of Instinct?

The problem of the maintenance of the Race has been solved under the method of Instinct by the possession of certain inborn impulses, inherited and transmissible, leading to the perpetuation of the species. Instinct, that is, transmutes, in the mind of the individual animal, that which in reality is essential to racial survival into the gratification of the immediate impulse.

To the purely instinctive animal, his real interest is all unknown. Knowing nothing beyond his impulse, he is wholly dominated by it: the gratification may or may not be to his own ultimate advantage, but such a doubt cannot rise above a mental horizon that is bounded by Instinct. Instinct leaves no judgment to the Individual: the impulse is inborn and is unquestionable. Thus regarded, it will be seen that Instinct is purely an appurtenance of the Race, acts in the interest of the Race, is inherited by every generation, and again transmitted, securing the subordination of the Individual to the Race. An individual end appears to be sought, but a racial end is in reality achieved. Its advantages belong to the Race. But what are its disadvantages? How—as apart from the species or the Race—does the Individual himself fare? How far is his interest consulted, not in appearance but in reality, under the method of Instinct? Let us take the more highly organised species as more relative to our present argument. There we find that every individual is impelled, by an Instinct over which he can exercise no control, to the care of the young of the species. The point that it is important here to note is that, beyond the gratification of the parental Instinct, the adult individual is in no way advantaged by these labours. Probably the study of the domesticated animals, by whom we are chiefly surrounded, gives us no adequate measure of the severity of these labours as they exist, let us say, in the jungle. Certainly it can give us no measure of the dangers and sufferings there incurred at the bidding of this

THE METHOD OF INSTINCT 15

tyrannous Instinct. Yet anyone who has watched a pair of martins, under our own eaves, feeding their young brood, persuading them to fly, and preparing them for their migration, can form some conception of it. The young beaks are incessantly open and clamorous. Through the livelong day the parents, thin, and working to the point of exhaustion, must hunt for the sake of the insatiable young. This is repeated year after year, throughout the life of the parents, and generation after generation takes up the labour. The parents are but the tools of the Instinct that is the possession of the Race. Again the advantage of Instinct falls wholly to the Race; but here there is a definite disadvantage to the Individual: he is deceived by the gratification of an inborn impulse. His true individual interest does not enter into the scheme at all.

But this instinctive subordination of the Individual to the Race has a further effect, an effect in which we can trace the sacrifice of the Individual in favour of the Race upon a yet greater scale.

As a result of the operation of the two instincts to which we have referred, the animal world brings forth and rears its kind in numbers that far exceed the limits of possible sustenance. Thus, these labours, already so costly to the Individual, bring about and maintain at a maximum the most ruthless competition. The struggle for life begins soon after life itself, and thereafter knows no respite. As Sir E. Ray Lankester says,[1] in speak-

[1] *Kingdom of Man*, p. 11. Constable & Co., London, 1907.

ing of the stress of competition in the animal world: "The earth's surface is practically full, that is to say, fully occupied. Only one pair can grow up to take the place of the pair—male and female—which have launched a dozen, or it may be as many as a hundred thousand young individuals on the world. . . . Animal population does not increase." The animal world, then, has long ago reached the limit of possible sustenance: its numbers cannot increase. Thus, while Instinct leads to the most rapid reproduction that is possible to any given species, and moreover subordinates the lives of the parents to the rearing of the young who are brought forth in such profusion, only one pair can grow up and succeed to the position of their parents. In this multitude of young no two will be absolutely alike: all will vary more or less from one another. As the competition is for the absolute necessities of life, the actual struggle is *inter se* among the young of every species. The result is that those two who reach adult life and take the place of their parents are the two whose variations have fitted them most accurately for the circumstances under which they will have to live. The enormous majority die before the age of parenthood is reached, and leave no mark upon the future of their race. A tiny minority, a chosen band selected by the accuracy of their adaptation to their surroundings, alone survives, and through them alone the Race is continued.

It is difficult to realise the awful severity of the conditions that thus come into existence, but

THE METHOD OF INSTINCT

it is easily perceived that the end secured is the organic advance and perfection of the Race. Once again, this racial advantage is achieved at the cost of the Individual. The method of Instinct not only condemns individuals, after a brief glimpse of life, to die in myriads, but exposes the survivors to a competition that is internecine and lifelong. We find that, under this method, all the advantages are made over to the Race; the suffering and the effort to the Individual. We find that this suffering shows itself in two forms, the first being the stress involved in the rearing of the young of the species, and the second, consequent upon the first, being the stress involved in the competition for life. By force of his inherited and inborn impulses the Individual is held in subjugation to the Race, and thus Instinct, answering the riddle of the Sphinx, brings about the co-ordination of the transitory and the permanent.

Leaving this aspect of the subject, we have to go a step further, and to ask whether a method that is so costly to the Individual is not imperfect, inherently and in itself? Is all this suffering inevitable, or can we discover an underlying flaw—the cause of its imperfection?

Such a flaw is to be found in its waste of effort—a wastefulness that is practically without a limit. The myriads of the slain are the product of the stress of ages; immeasurable effort has been expended on their evolution, and yet they are cast away as worthless. The history of progress by the method of Instinct is the record of a wastefulness that is beyond our powers of conception.

Nevertheless, this wastefulness is inevitable; it is necessarily inherent in the instinctive method. When we grant the method, then we find that there is no violation of the well-recognised parsimony of nature. The result is the best that the method will admit. The flaw is in the method. To throw light upon this point we must ask the question: "What can we discern in the method itself that has necessitated the destruction of life that has gone on everywhere throughout the ages?"

In the vegetable world it is clear that the waste is inevitable—that those among whom it occurs have not any possible means of learning to avoid it. To the plant, experience is a word of no meaning —advance is only possible by survival of the best-adapted variety, and destruction of the remainder.

Neither does pure Instinct—great as are its advantages—provide any escape from this necessity. To the purely instinctive animal, as to the plant, experience is still a word of no meaning. As we have seen, his impulses are inborn and unquestionable. He is constructed to live or die according to their efficiency. They are inherited; they belong to the Race; no possible personal experience can dictate to him his course of action. Instinct alone speaks in the imperative mood.

Perhaps our meaning will be most happily illustrated by the following observation, recorded by Darwin:[1] "Another and smaller species of Fur-

---

[1] *Journal of Researches into the Natural History and Geology of the Countries visited during the Voyage of H.M.S. "Beagle" round the World*, pp. 95 *et seq.* Murray, London, 1870.

narius (*F. Cenicularius*) resembles the oven-bird. . . . From its affinity the Spaniards call it 'casarita' (or little house-builder), although its nidification is quite different. The casarita builds its nest at the bottom of a narrow cylindrical hole, which is said to extend horizontally to nearly six feet underground. Several of the country people told me that, when boys, they had attempted to dig out the nest, but had scarcely ever succeeded in getting to the end of the passage. The bird chooses any low bank of firm sandy soil by the side of a road or stream. Here (at Bahia Blanca) the walls round the houses are built of hardened mud; and I noticed one, which enclosed a courtyard where I lodged, was bored through by round holes in a score of places. On asking the owner the cause of this, he bitterly complained of the little casarita, several of which I afterwards observed at work. It is rather curious to find how incapable these birds must be of acquiring any notion of thickness, for although they were constantly flitting over the low wall, they continued vainly to bore through it, thinking it an excellent bank for their nests. I do not doubt that each bird, as often as it came to daylight on the opposite side, was greatly surprised at the marvellous fact."

Here is an example of the limitation of Instinct—the flaw that involves the wastefulness of the method. The casarita—and we may take her case as typical—was entirely obedient to Instinct. Yet for want of the faculty of drawing inferences—in a word, from the want of Reason—she failed in her attempt at such an essential as nidification. She flitted to and fro across the wall, saw how thin it was, but could not draw the inference that a tunnel driven into it would merely lead to daylight again, and that an attempt at nesting there would be labour in vain. Her instinct was followed blindly. Her faculties did not include the power of drawing inferences, and so experience was of no value to her. The waste that was going on was inevitable, and inherent in the method under which she worked.

It will, however, be said that many of the animals that we know do possess, in a certain degree, the power of reasoning, and that we are overstating their helplessness. This is not only true, but is a fact of the most profound significance. The animals that we know are those who have emerged victorious from ages of competition so vast that they can only be expressed in terms of geological time. We have some grounds for a belief that the destructiveness of what we have called the flaw in Instinct was operative on a far greater scale in the past, and that the animals with whom we are acquainted have been the survivors, just in virtue of the possession of this modicum of Reason. It is probable that a purely instinctive fauna disappeared before the onset of the very beginnings of Reason, unable to live in the presence of the competition of animals whose methods were, to a greater or lesser degree, not so " wasteful " as their own.

Thus Sir E. Ray Lankester, F.R.S., writes:[1] " The extinct mammals Titanotherium and Dino-

[1] *Extinct Animals*, p. 209. A. Constable & Co., 1905.

ceras have brains one-eighth the bulk of living mammals the same size, such as rhinoceros and hippopotamus. So it was with the huge extinct reptiles. In some the head itself was ridiculously small according to our notions of customary proportion, and even in others, such as Triceratops, when the bony and muscular parts were big, as in rhinoceros, yet the brain was incredibly small. It could have been passed all along the spinal canal in which the spinal cord lies, and was in proportion to bulk of body a tenth the size of that of a crocodile."

We may fairly attribute to the small-brained creatures of past geological periods an existence that, to all intents and purposes, was entirely instinctive in character. Their extinction seems to have coincided in point of time with the earliest appearance of the larger-brained creatures who became the primitive ancestors of the animals that we see around us to-day. There was a "fault" in the line of descent, and a fresh start was made. The small-brained—the flying lizards and their congeners—became extinct, and, with few exceptions, they were not the ancestors of our present fauna. These exceptions, of which we may take the elephant as an example, are also instructive, for they appear to have developed an increased size of the brain at the same period, and thus to have escaped extinction. In every case the victory of survival passed to the larger-brained animals whose descendants we know.

Furthermore, we have to recognise that these, their descendants, possess not only the larger brain, but also a tincture of Reason. We may justly infer that some such tincture went with the larger brain among their ancestors—that the victory was due to this and to the less "wasteful" method of life that came with it. To quote Sir E. Ray Lankester again:[1] "It is a very striking fact that it was not in the ancestors of man alone that this increase in the size of the brain took place at this period, viz. the Miocene. ... It seems that we have to imagine that the adaptation of mammalian form to the various conditions of life had in Miocene times reached a point when further alteration and elaboration of the various types which we know existed could lead to no advantage. The variations presented in the struggle for existence presented no advantage—the 'fittest' had practically been reached, and continued to survive with little change. Assuming such a relative lull in the development of mere mechanical form, it is obvious that the opportunity for those individuals with the most 'educable' brains to defeat their competitors would arise. No marked improvement in the instrument being possible, the reward, the triumph, the survival would fall to those who possessed most skill in the use of the instrument. And in successive generations the bigger and more educable brains would survive and mate, and thus bigger and bigger brains would be produced." This movement—the movement in the direction of the power of drawing inferences—in the direc-

[1] *The Kingdom of Man*, pp. 22 *et seq.* Constable & Co., London, 1907.

THE METHOD OF INSTINCT 23

tion of filling up the gap in Instinct that was seen by Darwin in the action of the casarita—has already gone far. This may be illustrated in the most interesting manner by the feats of the Arctic Fox, recorded as follows by Dr. Romanes:[1] "I have previously published the facts in my lecture before the British Association in 1879, and therefore shall here quote from it. Desiring to obtain some Arctic Foxes, Dr. Rae set various kinds of traps: but as the foxes knew these traps from previous experience, he was unsuccessful. Accordingly he set a trap with which the foxes in that part of the country were not acquainted. This consisted of a loaded gun set upon a stand pointing at the bait. A string connected the trigger of the gun with the bait, so that when the fox seized the bait he discharged the gun, and thus committed suicide. In this arrangement the gun was separated from the bait by a distance of about thirty yards, and the string which connected the trigger with the bait was concealed throughout nearly its whole distance in the snow. The gun-trap thus set was successful in killing one fox, but never in killing a second, for the foxes afterwards adopted either of two devices whereby to secure the bait without injuring themselves. One of them was to bite through the string at its exposed part near the trigger; and the other was to burrow up to the bait through the snow at right angles to the line of fire, so that,

---

[1] *Animal Intelligence*, pp. 429 et seq., by George Romanes, LL.D., F.R.S. Vol. xli. of International Science Series. Kegan Paul, Trench & Co., 1882.

although in this way they discharged the gun, they escaped with perhaps only a pellet or two in the nose. Now both of these devices exhibited a wonderful degree of what I think must fairly be called reasoning."

The conclusion is indisputable.

Fox No. 1 is shot from a distance of thirty yards. And, although it is not stated as a fact, we may assume that the occurrence was watched by Fox No. 2, and that it was unprecedented in his experience. Nevertheless he is able to draw several inferences from the facts before him. *A.* He infers that the explosion is caused by pulling the string. *B.* Thence he infers that, if he severs the string, he may safely take the bait. *C.* He also infers that the only point at which he may safely gnaw through the string is behind the place where the explosion appeared, that is, near the trigger. Fox No. 3 has also watched, and makes the inference that, if he seizes the bait from below, he will be out of the line of danger.

This is a clear example of the avoidance of the " wastefulness " of pure Instinct. Fox No. 2 and Fox No. 3 survive, not in virtue of any variation of form, but because they were able to draw inferences from their recent experience.

This brings us definitely to Reason. The animal survivors from past epochs are those in whom we can see a new faculty arising to remedy the defect in Instinct. Just as, near the bottom of the ladder, the power of inborn instinctive action has been added to Reflex Power, so the power of rational action—action, that is, which is based upon the

THE METHOD OF INSTINCT

faculty of drawing inferences—has been superadded to Instinct.

The instinctive method of life has been successful in subordinating the Individual to the Race, but owing to its wastefulness it is being superseded by another. The method that follows may be a brilliant gain in every other way, but, if it fails to enable that which is passing to act on behalf of that which is permanent, no method, no species, no race, no civilisation or empire can endure.

Thus, the issue before us is tremendous, for we now pass on to consider the sufficiency of the method of pure Reason.

CHAPTER III

THE METHOD OF REASON

Mr. Herbert Spencer, in his *Data of Ethics*, chaps. xiii. and xiv., while recognising the defects of existing human nature, nevertheless looks forward to a time when the survival, in the matter of parenthood, of those who show the greatest disposition to subordinate their own interests to the interests of the race shall have led to the evolution of a society in which the individuals will find their greatest pleasure in that subordination. An improved or perfected human nature is to emerge, in which this subordination, necessarily instinctive in character, will be accompanied by a sense of gratification analogous to that which obtains among the higher animals when the parent subordinates himself to the nurture and protection of his young.

It is evident that this view assumes the drift and tendency of human evolution to be still in the direction of an ever closer approximation towards the perfection of the method of Instinct.

This method would become impossibly cumbrous were it asked to provide an impulse that would spring into useful action in every emergency, and with every change of environment. But the power of drawing inferences provides a short-cut to a position that, without being cumbrous, is

THE METHOD OF REASON

equally advantageous. It is the appearance of a new invention, working by a new method.

Mr. Spencer's view ignores the evolutionary value and ever-increasing power of Reason as compared with Instinct. It ignores the fact that, granted a sufficiently long continuance of this relative rate of growth, a time must come when their relative positions will be reversed—when Reason will have overtaken Instinct—when Reason will no longer be the slave, subservient to the gratification of the impulses of Instinct, but will take precedence as the master, holding those impulses under control. It ignores the obvious reflection that an animal thus endowed with uncontrolled power of rational action would presently make himself the master of the world, and that the gulf between him, the primarily rational, and the others, the primarily instinctive, would be so enormous that the disparity would appear to be one of kind rather than of degree. If we recognise that the human being has become the overlord of creation, we must also recognise that his position is itself due to the fact that, in him, Reason has at last attained the overlordship over Instinct.

The immensity of the power that is conferred by this faculty is seen in the position that man, pre-eminently the reasoning animal, holds as contrasted with the rest of the organic world. Except in this particular—the power of drawing a conclusion from premisses—he is the feeblest of all the more highly organised creatures. His skin is unprotected, he is atrophied in tooth and claw, and he is not even possessed of speed in flight. As has been pointed out in an article in the *Spectator*, the syllogism has become his only sword and his only shield. Yet his magnificent power of drawing inferences has placed him at the head of the organic world, and the splendour of his achievements shines in history.

Nevertheless, if his dependence upon Reason is thus absolute, if that is to be his only support, then the method of Reason, unlike the method of Instinct, should have no inherent flaw—else, as his position is exalted, so also must it be precarious. His method must, that is, have no racial inadequacy, for, in the alternative, all purely rational civilisations, one after another, are foredoomed to decay.

The shadows of history, not less marked than its splendours, suggest that there is in the background the possibility of inherent limitation—of something transient—in the value of that method.

We shall use the words "Reason" or "pure Reason" to connote the power of drawing inferences—the logical faculty, untouched by Instinct from below, and dissociated from the Religious Motive above it. This may seem wilfully to disregard two obvious objections: firstly, that Reason does not exist as divorced from Instinct even among the most civilised men; and secondly, that Reason is generally found in conjunction with some form or other of Religious Motive. We can only refer the reader to what we have already pointed out when we compared recorded history to the resultant in the parallelogram of forces. Our object is to discover the value of the components.

THE METHOD OF REASON 29

If recorded history—if the world around us—is regarded as a complex of Instinct, Reason, and Religious Motive, and if our object is to discover the values of these components, then it is evident that the proposed distinction is justified.

It will be remembered that, when writing of Instinct, we pointed out that it was essentially a property of the Race; not necessarily acting to the advantage of the individual animal, but securing his subordination to the interests of the species. We saw that the gratification of his impulse was the lure that led him on: we saw the Race acting in its own interest by means of these impulses, and using the Individual as an instrument.

How do these things stand when we compare the method of Reason—the method of humanity—with this, the method of Instinct?

In the first place, we find that we have not to deal with a stereotyped inheritance such as Instinct. The rational being has attained the power of "looking before and after," and is able to discern in what direction an "enlightened self-interest" does in fact lead him during his own lifetime. The advantage of the power of drawing inferences is not limited to the Race, as is the advantage of the foregone conclusions of inborn impulse. The scope of Reason is wide. It is the Individual himself who reviews his circumstances, and who draws his own inference. The advantage conferred by Reason stands continuously and inevitably at the service of him who determines his own course of action by its means—it waits, that is, at the service of the Individual. Thus pure Reason does not, *per se*, subordinate its owner to any considerations outside his own interest. With the supersession of Instinct, and the appearance of the new *régime*, the supreme power passes from the Race to the Individual.

In the second place, just as the purely reflex world knows nothing of inborn impulse, and the purely instinctive world knows nothing of inference, so it is only in the world of Reason that the possibility of conduct that is to the ultimate interest of the Individual appears upon the scene. Inferential conduct stands in the same relation to Reason as action springing from impulse stands to Instinct. Thus it comes about that, just as in dealing with Instinct we spoke of action springing from impulse, so now, in dealing with Reason, we shall have to speak of action springing from the inferences of the Individual—that is, of self-interested action, or "interest."

Reason, acting in the interest of the Individual, has modified already, and profoundly, the competitive stress of human life as compared with that which obtains among animals. We have already seen (page 16) that, in the world of Instinct, reproduction outruns the limits of possible sustenance, and that multiplication has long ago anticipated the whole supply of nourishment. Animal numbers cannot increase, and yet Instinct, careless of the fact, still carries on the work of reproduction at the highest pressure.

Among ourselves, Reason has actually reversed these conditions. We have no experience of the desperate efforts whereby life is maintained in the

THE METHOD OF REASON 31

jungle or in the ocean. The animal is dependent upon the food that it finds. Man, drawing an inference from his observation of the processes of nature, sows the seed and reaps the harvest. His gift of Reason is the true means whereby he subdues the jungle and the desert, and discovers vast areas, fertile and unoccupied, that await his coming. To him the possible limits of sustenance outrun reproduction.

Nevertheless, to man also, the two essential stresses of life remain unaltered. They are permanent elements in life, although the severity of the stress may be relieved. The kaleidoscope of existence has been turned, and the picture has changed; but it is still made up of the same pieces of glass. The possible supply of food may have outrun reproduction; unoccupied areas may await coming generations; but in life, as we know it, the stress still arises from the same two causes that are operative in the world of Instinct. These are still, firstly, the competition existing among those contemporaries to whom the present belongs, and, secondly, the effort and self-denial required in the nurture and care of our children, to whom the future belongs.

Evidently then, the question arises: "How will Reason, having already thus modified these permanent stresses, next proceed to deal with them?"

The rational manner in which these two stresses might be relieved has been in the past, and is at present, the subject of much speculation. When we survey this speculation broadly, we encounter two schools of thought. Each school, recognising the evils that would attend the abolition of one of these stresses, urges the abolition or modification of the other, in order that the incidence of the first might be made more tolerable. But the two schools are at variance on the question: " Which is the stress that should be modified, in order to make the burden of the other more tolerable?"

One of them, the older school, recognising the strain upon the Individual that is caused by competition, urges that it would become more tolerable if the reproductive activity of the Race were modified and lessened. The other, the newer school, recognising the racial evils and dangers attendant upon a low birthrate, urges the abolition of the competitive system of life, not only to secure relief from the stress involved, but also in order that the provision of future generations may be less burdensome.

Clearly we have to examine separately the incidence of these two stresses, and to determine the purely rational manner of dealing with them. In each case, as we have already shown, pure Reason must advance along the lines indicated by the interest of the Individual, for the supreme power belongs to him.

We ask therefore, alike with regard to the stress of competition and the stress of reproduction: " Whither do his interests lead him?"

Here it is necessary to guard ourselves against a verbal confusion that might easily lead to confusion of thought. The term " Individual" needs no definition, but the case is otherwise with the

THE METHOD OF REASON

words "Society" and "the Race." These terms are equally open to connote the sum of existing individuals; the, as yet, unborn generations of the future; or both together. As commonly used, the terms stand for at least two distinct ideas.

In considering the interest of the individual in relation to that of unborn generations we shall have frequent occasion to use the words "Society" and "Race." It is well, therefore, to define the precise meaning that will be attached to these words. We have reserved, and shall reserve, the word "Society" to express the sum of individuals co-existing at any given time, and the word "Race" to express the sum of the, as yet, unborn generations. This use of these words "Society" and "Race" will be rigidly adhered to, for the distinction will be found to be one of capital importance.

It will be noticed that the conception of Society, in the sense in which we are using the word, is the offspring of Reason, and unknown amid the uses of Instinct. In the region of Instinct we find only the Individual and the Race: even the herd is an institution of racial utility, while racial ideas are explicitly shut out from the meaning that we attach to the word "Society." Thus, with the advent of Reason, a new idea—a new factor—comes before us, to which due place must be given, and we shall have to consider the interaction of the interest of the Individual with the interest of Society, as well as with the interest of the Race.

And here a most interesting position is revealed, for we find that the consideration of the relative interests of the Individual and Society resolves itself into the examination of the stress of competition, just as does the consideration of the relative interests of the Individual and the Race resolve itself into the examination of the stress of reproduction.

It is evident that it is in contact with Society —and with Society alone—that the Individual incurs the stress of competition; the rivalry, that is, between any given individual and those, his contemporaries, who compete with him. In a word, the competitive stress divides the interest of the Individual, not from that of the Race, but from that of Society. In the same manner it is evidently in the matter of reproduction—and of reproduction alone—that the Individual and the Race come into contact with one another. The other stress, that of competition, does not enter, for it would be absurd to regard the existing individual as in a state of competition with generations that are yet to come. In a word, the reproductive stress separates the interest of the Individual, not from that of Society, but from that of the Race.

The first of the two succeeding chapters (Chap. IV) will be devoted to the consideration of the interest of the Individual, so far as social competition is concerned, and the next (Chap. V) to the consideration of the interest of the Individual, so far as the reproduction of the Race is concerned. In each case, Reason being at the service of the Individual, we shall have to answer the questions: " In what direction will the Individual be carried

THE METHOD OF REASON 35

by a strictly rational regard for his own interest? Can he eliminate these two separate stresses from his experience in life?"

After that, in the third succeeding chapter (Chap. VI), we shall undertake an estimation of the relative importance of the two conclusions that we shall have reached, and, in doing so, our attention will be engaged by finding that this discussion resolves itself into the consideration of the relative interests of Society and the Race, and that we have to decide, to the advantage of the Individual, between their claims to precedence.

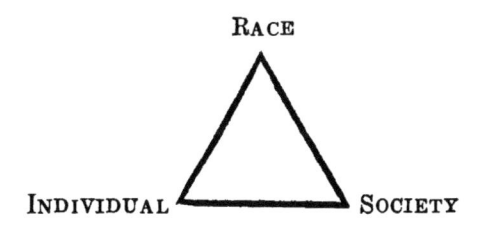

```
                    RACE
                     /\
                    /  \
                   /    \
                  /      \
         INDIVIDUAL------SOCIETY
```

We shall then, in the fourth succeeding chapter (Chap. VII), be in a position to review all the ground before us, under this, the *régime* of Reason, and to ask whether, considering the nature of the conclusion reached, the method of pure Reason can be justified. Pure Reason itself will come up for judgment. If, in the last analysis, the rational interests of the Individual are not found to be concurrent with the advantage of the Race; if, that is, they are not found to afford a sufficient basis for a stable civilisation, then we shall begin to understand the failures recorded in history, and the vaunted method of pure Reason will stand condemned.

CHAPTER IV

REASON IN RELATION TO COMPETITION: THE INTEREST OF THE INDIVIDUAL IN RELATION TO SOCIETY

SOCIETY, thus defined, may be regarded as an organism with, as it were, the same expectation of life as the average Individual. In point of duration in time there is no disparity between them.

How does the fact of this equality affect their relative interests? Evidently it dominates the situation. If the interests of both are confined within the same space of time, if there be no need to make provision for a future that neither will see—that is, if there is no occasion for present self-denial—then their interests will not be at variance by any antecedent necessity; they may be capable of reconciliation, and pure Reason may be a sufficient guide.

It will be observed that the interest of the Race is in no way involved herein. We have already seen that the reconciliation of the interest of the Individual with that of Society would only require the abolition of competition. We have, then, to deal only with the problem of the abolition of competition, and it is incumbent upon us to do so from a purely rational point of view, eliminating all that is either instinctive or disinterested.

What has been hitherto the action of Reason

INDIVIDUAL AND SOCIETY 37

in dealing with the strife between any given individual and the society that surrounds him?

We have already pointed out (pp. 30 *et seq.*) that it has been in the direction of modifying and softening this rivalry, and that it has done so with such effect that we are able to increase in numbers, and know little or nothing of the wastefulness and severity that obtain under Instinct, and make competition there an internecine contest for dear life itself. Nor do we see any prospect of a return to this state of things. Are we threatened by any material appreciation in the value of food? The chemical fixation of nitrogen may be accomplished. Are we threatened by a failure of fuel? We have the prospect of being able to unlock the boundless stores of intra-atomic energy.

The power of Reason is so great, indeed, that the prospect before us is one in which we see the probability of moving yet further away from the severity of instinctive conditions. Resulting from the rational faculty, the movement itself is evolutionary in character, and can be stayed only by a faculty even more commanding than Reason. Already the competition that we have to consider, both now and in the prospect before us, is no longer for the possession of life itself, but for those possessions that seem to make life of value.

Although this immense change has already been wrought by Reason, nevertheless the interest of the Individual is still at variance with that of his fellows, the rivalry of life still continues, and competition is still one of the two great factors of the stress that is the experience of every one.

But why should Reason rest content with this modification? Why should it stop with its work half done? Why should it not devote itself to the complete cessation of the competitive stress, and to the substitution of a non-competitive system of life? Reason, as we have seen, first achieved its predominance by reducing the limitless wastefulness that is inherent in the method of Instinct. It is in this direction that Reason is still operative, and the two questions arise: " Is it to the interest of the Individual to abolish competition?" and then, if that be answered in the affirmative, we have to ask: " Is it in his power to abolish competition? Is Reason competent to secure this end?"

In answering the first of these questions, we find the assertion that the elimination of the competitive struggle would be an advantage is met by dissent, and frequently by a sense of horror. This feeling is found not only among the successful—the "haves" as opposed to the unsuccessful, the "have-nots"—it is found also among the "have-nots"; it overrides the distinction of class. It is not, even among the "haves," primarily a selfish feeling. On the contrary, as a matter of fact, it is found especially and essentially among the least selfish members of the community. It speaks with power and conviction, and, in its presence, Reason seems to have lost some of its old-time cogency. The authority of Reason is not weakened, and yet, when all is admitted, it does not prevail against the sentiment of aversion.

We shall find the explanation in the fact that the present chapter is concerned only with the method of Reason—the method that judges by interest. When tested by the standard of interest, a non-competitive form of society satisfies every requirement. It is only when, in a later chapter, we come to measure it by another standard—a standard of which interest knows nothing—that we shall find our horror is justified.

As we might expect under these circumstances, when we examine the arguments put forward by those who, professedly on the ground of interest, are the opponents of the demand for the elimination of competition, we find that they are rather the expression of this sentiment of aversion than a logical demonstration of any irrational quality in that demand.

Thus it has been urged by many that the defeets of existing human nature are such as, in the absence of competition, would create evils far greater and less remediable than those of which all men disapprove in the existing arrangements of the world. Of such evils, slavery is instanced. The defects of existing human nature, it is said, are such that, in the absence of the stimulus of competition, the necessary work of Society could only be carried on by the rule of a disciplined army of civil officials. Before them, the wishes of any Individual would be as nought in comparison with the claims of Society, and the final result would be a revival of despotism in the form of bureaucracy.

This is undisputable. But, in the first place, we must point out that the incubus of a defective human nature is a constant element in any form of Society. If we compare any competitive form with any non-competitive form, it is a weight that is present in both scales of the balance. In the second place, it will be seen that by the proposed co-ordination of the work that is necessary to carry on Society, an economy of effort would be secured; and that Reason would be pursuing its old course. In other words, the slavery involved would be less than the aggregate of servitude that is inevitable if the despot is competition itself—the servitude that is inherent in the very idea of competition among a multitude of individuals. Friction leads to an inevitable waste of energy in the working of any machine, but the loss is greater in proportion to the number of bearings through which it is distributed. Thus, from a purely interested point of view, it is better to serve a despotic bureaucracy, than to live in competition with all the members of surrounding Society.

That all objections, such as this concerning slavery, are brought forward in good faith is unquestionable. But it is also unquestionable that the aversion felt is stronger than the arguments that seek to justify it. The revulsion of feeling arises, in fact, from a negation that is deeper and wider than any argument based upon interest—a negation whose real character is generally unrecognised in the minds of the writers.

Another class of objectors urges that, even though a non-competitive society were successful in reducing its internal friction to a minimum, still it would be only the material welfare and æsthetic enjoyment of its members that would

INDIVIDUAL AND SOCIETY

be secured, and that, not indeed an organic change, but a profound degeneration of individual character would be the result. It is urged that, as Herbert Spencer says,[1] "The welfare of a society and the justice of its arrangements are at bottom dependent on the character of its members."

This again is indisputable. But, considered in a strictly rational manner, it will be seen that it is begging the question. The character of the members of a non-competitive community, however degenerate and contemptible, in the absence of the stimulus of competition, it might become from our point of view, would be exactly the character necessary for the welfare and smooth working of such a society. All that it requires is a purely rational character, looking only and strictly to material welfare and æsthetic enjoyment. Anything beyond would create friction in such a society, until, in the presence of its despotism, it had undergone the atrophy of disuse. The unselfish and self-reliant qualities, alike essential to any form of competitive society, would not only cease to be essential, they would be detrimental, and a "degenerate" character would be the essential. Degeneration of character as we esteem it—yes, hopeless degeneration as we esteem it. Considered, however, in its strictly rational aspect, such a degeneration of character is not to be regarded as an objection.

Yet when we speak of such "degeneration" we are again brought back to the revulsion of feeling to which we have already referred. It is

[1] *The Man versus the State*, p. 39. Watts & Co., London, 1909.

a sentiment from which we cannot escape. To admit that it is irrational is not to remove it. Indeed, the more nakedly the rational character of a non-competitive society is exposed, the more intense is the revulsion that it inspires.

This attitude of dissent, being supra-rational in quality, cannot be removed by purely rational considerations. It is dictated and enforced by a power superimposed over that of pure Reason. The nature and indispensability of this power, superior to that of pure Reason, will be discussed later: its intervention is not admissible while we are discussing the method of Reason. For the present it is enough to have shown that the denials of the advantage of a liberation from competition are in truth based upon this, and that therefore, in pure Reason, they are not to the point. Nowhere do they traverse the obvious fact that, carrying the work of Reason to its logical conclusion, an entire relief from the incubus of competition would be to the interest of every individual. The considerations of pure Reason, that is to say, lead us to the conclusion that the elimination of competition, if possible, would serve alike the interest of the Individual and of Society.

Seeing, then, that it is genuinely to the interest of the Individual to abolish competition, we ask at once: "Is it in his power to do so? Is it possible?"

You cannot get rid of competition except by getting rid of that for the sake of which competition is carried on. Individual ownership of the

INDIVIDUAL AND SOCIETY

things that seem to make life worth living is evidently the stumbling-block in the way of the realisation of this object. The runners compete for a prize. To put an end to the stress of the race, to reduce it to a walk-over that shall be a strain upon none, the prize must not go to any one of them. It must be the acquisition of all, and owned equally.

The economic system which proposes that collective ownership should be substituted for private property is known at the present moment by the name of "Socialism," and the ordinary phrase by which it is defined is "the common ownership of all the means of production, distribution, and exchange." It is also spoken of as "nationalisation" of all property.

Under such a system—one, that is, excluding private possession and recognising only common ownership—it is evident that the reward of all labour would be for use in common, and that it would profit the individual labourer only indirectly, and by advancing the community of which he was a member. All work of head or hand would but contribute to the common good, and serve to maintain or raise the general standard of living. Competition would have become objectless.

It has been urged that it is not within the power of Reason to bring about such a change in our environment. It is pointed out that, according to a condition that has been in force from the beginning of life onwards, life itself has been held only as the reward of success in competition; that there are but few exceptions to this condition in the tenure of life, and that we owe all advance to its operation. Furthermore, the system of individual ownership of property, whether instinctive or rational, is antecedent to any form of human organisation. Thus, in Iceland, the many small lakes surrounding the large sheet of water known as Arnevatn are each occupied by one pair of swans (*Cygnus musicus*), who are always ready to fight ferociously with an intruder from one of the other lakes. Arnevatn itself is mapped out by invisible boundaries into areas that are each occupied by a single pair of swans, and trespass is invariably treated as a *casus belli*. Such examples of individual ownership antedating any form of human organisation might easily be multiplied. This passion for individual ownership is to be ascribed immediately to competitive conditions of life; so immediate is the connection that we can scarcely disentangle the two. When the wild swans fight, we should call it an example of competition for life—or for the means of life. Probably the swans would call it a defence of the rights of property. Which would be correct? Both, for the two things go together. Under these circumstances it is urged that the impulse to competition and the tendency to individual ownership are among the most ancient and primitive instincts; that they are so far innate and ingrained that any form of human society, if it is to be successful, can be but the expression of them and secondary to them; and that all human social systems must ultimately stand or fall according to the measure of their harmony with these, their antecedents.

INDIVIDUAL AND SOCIETY

That there is great practical weight in this objection is not to be denied. But we must point out that the present pages are not devoted to the consideration of what is practical, but to the discovery of tendencies—to the discovery of the underlying forces that go to the formation of the practical resultant that we see, and to the recognition of their character as making for growth or decay.

Thus considered, we find that the above argument ignores the progressively increasing ascendancy of Reason, and its advancing efficiency in the prevention of waste of effort. In competition and private ownership we still retain much of the wastefulness of the primitive method of the instinctive world. Why are we to expect that so wasteful a method should be exempt from the inferential power of Reason? It must be remembered that we are travelling along a road, and not standing still. Such an appeal to Instinct is an appeal to the slave against his master, and, when the prepotent factor is no longer Instinct, but Reason, then all human social systems must ultimately come into being according to their success in the avoidance of waste, and the saving of internal friction that they achieve. If the impulse to competition and the tendency to individual ownership cannot justify themselves rationally, they cannot withstand this movement. Their wastefulness of effort precludes them from doing so.

When we look at the position still more closely we realise that common ownership would not only bring the competition between the Individual and Society to an end, but that the interest of the

Individual would be actually merged in and identified with that of Society. For if all things were owned in common, it is evident that a general equality would result, and continue so long as the system lasted. Under these circumstances a man could only find his private advantage in the improvement of the common good, and by sharing in the general rise in the standard of living that he has helped to bring about. And it would equally be to the interest of all other members of such a Society to seek their own purely selfish ends in the same manner—by seeking, that is, to raise the general standard of living in order that they might share therein. Thus the interests of the separate members of a non-competitive social machine could not rationally be diverse from one another: the amount of the friction of life would be reduced to an inevitable minimum. In proportion as the system were non-competitive so would be its efficiency in saving the waste of effort.

But we have seen that through ages of evolution it has been the office of Reason to prevent such waste: that it is in virtue of the energy thus set free that the rational world has secured its pre-eminence. Here, then, in the absolute identification of the interest of the Individual with that of Society, we recognise the maximum development and the highest expression of Reason.

The conclusion reached is, then, that pure Reason not only seeks the cessation of the stress involved in competition, but that it—the predominant partner in the association with Instinct—is competent to secure this end by the substitution

INDIVIDUAL AND SOCIETY 47

of common ownership for the existing system of private property. Furthermore, we conclude that this change would not only terminate the conflict between the Individual and Society, but would secure the absolute identification of their interests by a "social contract" that is as naturally and inevitably the outcome of the working of pure Reason as an instinctive action is the outcome of inborn impulse.

CHAPTER V

REASON IN RELATION TO REPRODUCTION: THE INTEREST OF THE INDIVIDUAL IN RELATION TO THE RACE.

WHEN the reader recalls what has already been put forward in these pages, he will readily see that racial advantage does not now concern us, because at present we are limited to the consideration of the matter strictly from the point of view of a purely rational individual. Purely rational conduct will be dictated solely by the prepotent interest of the Individual, and any result that may accrue to the Race will be merely incidental.

Thus, in the matter of reproduction, we can neither hark back to the Instincts that concern themselves about the Race, nor go forward to the consideration of any course of action founded upon a disinterested basis, and involving the subjection of the Individual to the interest of the Race. To do so would create a confusion of thought. It would be either infra-rational, that is, instinctive; or else it would be supra-rational.

In either case it would be extraneous at the present stage of our inquiry.

Therefore, just as when we were dealing with Reason in relation to the competitive or social stress, we asked, firstly: "Is it to the interest

INDIVIDUAL AND RACE

of the Individual to abolish competition?" and secondly: "Is it in his power to do so?" So now we ask, firstly: "Is it to the interest of the Individual to decline the provision of future generations?" and secondly: "Is it in his power to do so?"

Before we can answer the first of these questions we must deal with the possible objection that the question itself is unfair. It may be urged that the desire for offspring is so primitive and innate an instinct that it ought not to be excluded from consideration, that rational conduct is controlled by it, and that the Race will always be continued under its influence. This reliance on Instinct is, however, a racial parallel to the social dependence on it that was examined on page 45. Then we discussed the contention that a socialist form of Society was impossible because the tendency to individual ownership was so primitive and powerful an instinct that it would prevail even though irrational. Now we are discussing the contention that the desire for offspring is so powerful and primitive an instinct that it can defy the power of Reason.

In each case the answer is the same. Instinct subjects the Individual to a system of social competition and racial servitude. Reason frees him from both. Instinct and Reason pull in opposite directions, and their spontaneous co-operation is impossible. And Instinct wanes while Reason waxes. Ever more and more Instinct is held in the leash of Reason, and, in any rational society, a time inevitably comes when the relative increase in the power of Reason leads to the synchronous appearance of socialistic phenomena and a failure of the birthrate; a simultaneous yielding to the social stress and the racial stress to which reference will be made later on (page 61).

The Race may be regarded as an organism possessed, practically, of an indefinitely prolonged existence. The Individual, on the contrary, has but a brief span of life. The duration of his life, as compared with that of the existence of the Race, is almost negligible. The Race has been said to live in an "ever-moving present." The Individual lives in the presence of an ever-approaching Death. Death is the factor that draws the distinction between the two.

We are dealing with interests. How does this factor affect their respective interests? It is evident that if the Individual lived, or rather, expected to live, as long as the Race (and no increase in numbers took place), then, as in the case of the Individual and Society, their interests would march together, would be identical, and pure Reason a sufficient guide. In the absence of this factor, their interests need not, of any antecedent necessity, be the same.

> "Cuncta manus avidas fugient haeredis amice
> Quae dederis animo."
> —Hor., *Odes*, iv. 7.

> "All spent on your dear self will escape the greedy hands of your heir."

When a great estate is entailed, each successive "owner," although entitled to deal with the income, is under constraint to leave the capital undiminished and untouched. It is evident that the constraint is the essence of this arrangement. Let us look at such a case solely from the point of view of the "owner's" rational interests. Cut away from below him the purpose of the promptings of Instinct, erase from above him every disinterested motive, and what is his advantage in the continuance of the entail? What are the coming generations of the family to such a one? What, to him, is a future in which he has no part and no lot? It is postulated that he is moved only by individual interest. If he has the power to spend the capital upon himself; if the deterring constraint is removed; why should he resist the temptation to do so? The conclusion is inevitable. He would spend the capital within his own lifetime. And if he goes childless through life, nature inflicts no penalty either upon him or upon any other individual. But the Race is injured: the penalty of nature falls in the disappearance of the family.

When we turn to the facts of life we find that the parallel is exact. Let us assume—the assumption will not be very far wrong—that that part of the stress of life which is represented by the efforts of the Individual to maintain himself in competition with his contemporaries is equivalent to the part represented by the efforts necessary in the nurture, care, and education of the young, who belong to the coming generation. On this assumption, those—married or unmarried—who elect to go childless through life are relieved of one-half of the stress and anxiety that is the lot of those who have elected to be the parents of the generations to come. Whether our assumption of one-half as the measure of the relief is correct or not, is unimportant. The relief, the advantage in the competitive stress, is in any case enormous. The energy thus set free lays open the whole vista of life to such a one. Leisure, travel, adventure, all that the kingdoms of this world can offer, are his; and to marry, which is the great racial act of a man's lifetime, is the maddest and most irrational act that it is possible to conceive.

Thus, rationally, each sex is apt to regard the other as the cause of its own undoing; and we witness such a portent as the sex-antagonism that is now springing up.

Building up the future rests upon burdened shoulders; and those who are burdened are easily passed in the race. Thus, under a competitive system, it is clearly to the interest of the Individual to break the entail, and to spend upon himself all the riches of life. The hostility between the interests of the Individual and the Race that would exist among animals, were it not masked by Instinct, appears upon the scene uncovered in rational Society. Reason, *per se*, has no racial quality, it is not concerned to avert this hostility, and the distinction that Death draws between the Individual and the Race places their interests directly in opposition to one another.

If, then, it is to the interest of the life tenant to break the entail, the second of our two questions arises, and we must ask: "Is it in his power to do so?" Under Instinct the constraint that ensures the continuance of the entail of life is absolute.

INDIVIDUAL AND RACE 53

Does Reason not only lay bare the antagonism of interests, but also confer upon the Individual the power to act in his sole interest; the power, that is, to break the entail of life?

That it confers this power is incontestable. It is futile to say that Instinct, in this matter, still governs conduct, and that it shows little or no sign of weakening. The statement is quite true; but, strong as Instinct is, it has fallen into the toils of Reason, and is fooled of its purpose. There is no need to quote the figures issued by the British Registrar-General. In greater or less degree the fact is in evidence throughout every community of the white man. Moreover, in view of what has been pointed out above, it is interesting to observe that the birthrate falls, not only in direct ratio with the predominance of the rational faculty in any community, but also in a direct ratio with its comparative predominance in various classes of the same community. The spirit of the French mind is generally admitted to be the most logical and rational in Europe: France has the lowest birthrate. In America it has been noticed that the "Higher" education of women has had a striking effect in leading to avoidance of office—that is to say, in either preventing marriages, or in producing childless unions. Among ourselves the position is shown by the evidence given before the Royal Commission on Divorce, by Sir James Crichton-Browne, on 31st October 1910, when he said: "Since 1875 the average number of children produced by a fertile union has halved in the best families of all classes in this country."

The conclusion reached is, then, that pure Reason, careless of the Race, seeks the cessation of the self-sacrifice involved in parenthood. So far as the reproductive stress is concerned, the interests of the Individual and of the Race cannot be identified in pure Reason. In pure Reason the Individual is greater than the Race, and his interest prevails.

CHAPTER VI

RELATIVE INTEREST OF SOCIETY AND THE RACE UNDER THE METHOD OF REASON

IN the two preceding chapters we have considered the rational relations of the Individual and Society in the first, and of the Individual and the Race in the second. In the former we have seen that Reason desires, and can secure, the identification of the interest of the Individual with that of Society; in the latter we have seen that Reason is unsuccessful in a similar attempt upon the diverse interests of the Individual and the Race. It fails even to reconcile them, because Reason would subordinate the interest of the Race to that of the Individual. So we may summarise the matter by saying that, in the first case, the Individual is equal to Society, and that, in the second case, the Individual is greater than the Race.

Our next task is to examine the relation of the interest of Society with that of the Race, in order to complete the consideration of the triangle of interests that we have represented thus:

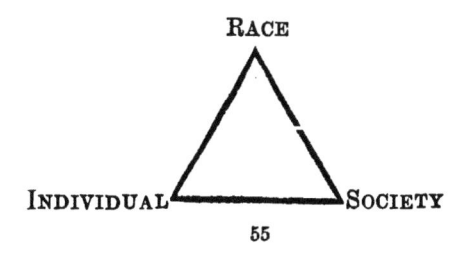

```
            RACE
             /\
            /  \
           /    \
          /      \
 INDIVIDUAL------SOCIETY
```

Now, if the interests of the Individual and Society are identical—if, that is, under a communistic system, Society takes the place of the Individual—then evidently the divergence between the interests of the Individual and the Race, which we noted, would appear, at first sight, also to involve a similar cleavage between the interests of Society and the Race. Whether this assumption will stand examination, or not, is the subject of the present stage of our inquiry.

It will be remembered that the failure of Reason to reconcile the interests of the Individual and the Race concerned the matter of reproduction. Applying here the same test, the question becomes: "Can Reason so state the terms of their mutual dependence that Society will find its interest in the encouragement of the reproduction and nurture of the Race?"

It is unquestionable that the older school of economists, referred to in Chap. III, were right when they urged that the strain upon the Individual, caused by competition, could be rendered more tolerable if the reproductive activity of the Race were lessened. It is equally obvious that the newer school is also right when, recognising the racial evils and dangers attendant upon a low birthrate, it urges alternatively that, the competitive system of life once abolished, the provision of future generations would become less burdensome. For, if Society, under a system of common ownership, took the place of the Individual, and shouldered the reproductive stress that is now borne by him, then the weight of the burden might be lessened, though only slightly, by unification of effort. So far as the unification were rational, it would save a certain amount of energy now wasted: just as the care of a hundred patients is more easily carried on in one hospital than in a hundred separate homes.

But these two contentions, however true, are equally beside the point. They juggle with the items in the face of bankruptcy. They are extraneous to the present argument, because they propose merely a reduction of the two stresses. Imperious Reason knows no such limitation, but demands their total abolition. She, moreover, has the power to secure these ends. To offer less is to palter with pure Reason. And pure Reason does not lend herself to equivocation. You cannot pick and choose. She demands, not that the binding rope which cuts into the flesh shall be loosened, but that it shall be removed altogether.

There is nothing here to show that it is less clearly to the interest of Society than of the Individual to check the work of reproduction. Indeed, under Socialism, the identification of the interest of the Individual with that of Society is not approximate, but absolute. It is not to the interest of a Socialistic Society to permit more than an irreducible minimum of reproduction on the part of the individuals composing it.

For, in a Socialistic Society in running order —a Society essentially contrived to secure material ease—is it to be imagined that the sense of the stress of reproduction, and of the costliness of the nurture of children, would not become more acute in proportion as the competitive stress is relieved? We have already pointed out that marriage would be an act of madness in a rational individual. Would multiplication be less than insanity on the part of a communist society?

Thus no system of common ownership, although it may remove the competitive stress, can remove the reproductive stress: it is not designed to that end. It may, perhaps, do something to mitigate the severity of its incidence, but it cannot, except by the avoidance of parenthood itself, effect the removal that is demanded by Reason. To the Individual it makes no material difference whether the stress falls upon him in the character of a father of a family, or in the character of a citizen of a Socialistic Society.

The purely rational demand would be that this stress should be removed, even as the competitive stress had been removed. We have seen already, that the Individual can only escape from this stress by the avoidance of parenthood itself. We see now, that a Socialistic Society fares no better. The logical position of Society, *vis-à-vis* to the Race, is the same as that of the Individual. The identity of their interests goes to the bitter end.

Moreover, if we regard a Socialistic, that is a non-competitive form of Society, as the most rational form, then it becomes evident, *à fortiori*, that it is an antecedent impossibility for any other form of rational Society, however constituted, or however reconstructed, to bridge the logical hiatus between its interest and that of the Race. Indeed, the more logically and rationally it is constructed, the more intrusive becomes the fact that the hostility between the interests of the Individual and the Race persists also into the relations between Society and the Race.

CHAPTER VII

THE CONDEMNATION OF THE METHOD OF REASON

IT is deeply interesting to note the manner in which the rational revolt against these two stresses, the social and the racial, occurs in the course of the growth of any modern civilisation. Practically always, the revolt shows itself at a certain stage of development, and the revolt against the one takes place nearly at the same time as the revolt against the other. We need not look far afield for an illustration of this coincidence. In English life the two outstanding features of the last quarter of a century are, the appearance of a Socialistic party, and a rapidly falling birthrate. Among ourselves, the tendency to a decline in the birthrate slightly preceded the Socialistic phenomena. In Germany, this order appears to have been reversed. German Socialism has, for some time past, been a powerful element in the composition of that empire, and yet there has been a great increase in the population. This, however, is at present mainly due to improved sanitary conditions, and the consequent preservation of the elderly. Already the German birthrate is falling rapidly. The "corrected" birthrate of Berlin in 1881 was 32·2, and in 1901 it was 26·8.[1]

[1] *The Declining Birthrate*, page 26, by Arthur Newsholme, M.D., Principal Officer of the Local Government Board. Cassell & Co. Ltd., 1911.

CONDEMNATION OF REASON 61

The nature of French genius ensured the appearance of the twin phenomena in France before they invaded England or Germany, but their advent coincided in point of time.

The cause of this simultaneity does not lie quite upon the surface; indeed, a tendency to demand common ownership and a tendency to limit reproduction appear, at first sight, to be dissimilar in character, and their coincidence to be fortuitous. Nevertheless, the cause of their conjunction will be sufficiently obvious to the reader of the preceding pages. Their common origin is to be found in the increasing preponderance of Reason, and the consequently increasing pursuit of self-interest. When that has reached a given point the effect becomes observable, both socially and racially.

We have seen that, even if the social stress had received its maximum of relief under a Socialistic organisation—the highest expression of Reason, in dealing with competition—still, the racial stress would be untouched, except by the rational destruction of the interest of the Race. It is therefore necessary, in the consideration of these twin phenomena, to devote ourselves to the examination of the one that is concerned with racial destruction at the bidding of Reason.

The power to control the birthrate—the power, that is, to break the entail of life—is wholly absent under the dispensation of Instinct; it is conferred by Reason alone, and therefore may be considered, from an evolutionary point of view, as a novel racial environment. Thus, the effects of this, not only the newest factor in evolution, but one of the first magnitude, are to be traced, not in the recesses of a tropical forest, but upon the highways of civilisation.

We have seen that Instinct, supervening over reflex power, was unable to do more, as in the case of the *casarita*, than follow the inborn impulse, whether it were self-destructive or not, under the circumstances of each individual case. Instinct, that is, was unable to dominate the environment that it had itself created when it supervened over merely reflex power. Instinct arose and survived, on account of its ability to deal advantageously with the conditions that had preceded it; that is to say, with quite another environment than that which it made for itself. In the result, it created an environment of limitless wastefulness—a wastefulness with which, for lack of the power of drawing inferences, it was itself unable to deal.

Even so it is with Reason in the matter of the birthrate. Reason arose and survived, on account of its power to deal advantageously with the wastefulness of the environment created by Instinct. But it is unable to dominate the new environment created by itself, or to remain within the boundaries of its usefulness. Thus, for example, to break the entail of life is the strict and inevitable work of pure Reason, for a rational society cannot stultify itself by refusing to make use of its power in a manner that has already been shown to be materially to the interest of all the living.

From an evolutionary point of view, it is impossible to exaggerate the importance of this new

CONDEMNATION OF REASON 63

racial environment. Its deadly character "leaps to the eye." The wastefulness of Instinct, unable to control the impulses that it created, finds its parallel in the wastefulness of Reason, obliged as it is to follow up in practice the inferences that it draws. In the former case, the individual lives are destroyed; in the latter, empire after empire and civilisation after civilisation are struck down. Reason magnifies its office, and, by the toll that it takes from the Race, becomes the instrument of ruin. Its pursuit of interest, so far as any power inherent in itself is concerned, is as uncontrollable as the impulses of pure Instinct; as fixed as the reflex response to a stimulus.

Even though we turn to the highest and most complete expression of interest—a communist form of society—still we find no logical foundation for permanence. We find, on the contrary, that a Socialistic Society is also automatically self-limiting, and lies open to the impact of the racial stress. We may, indeed, go further, and find, as a generalisation, that any civilisation must prove ephemeral in direct ratio to its dependence upon Reason. Where there is no place for disinterested conduct, there is no place for the child.

Lest such a conclusion should appear, even now, to be preposterous and unheard of, it may be well to illustrate our meaning by turning, for a moment, to facts that are within the cognisance of everyone, and we do this even though the time has not yet come for the discussion of the historical aspect of the subject.

In contemporary France, we may see the process in operation. But a very few generations have passed since the French held the hegemony of the world. At present, French Society, if not indeed Socialistic, is yet the Society from which non-rational considerations are more severely excluded than from any other. And the Frenchman is bound to the wheel of his own logical faculty. The most rational of beings, he perceives, indeed, the import of what is going on. Still, he is helpless, as though mesmerised, and wholly unable to suggest any rational means of averting the famine of children. The number and extent of his writings on *Dépopulation* testify that none can recognise his racial danger more clearly than he does, and yet he cannot draw back from it. On the contrary, Reason is compelling French Society to advance directly to the racial doom that its members see so plainly before them—the destruction that is their own act and deed—the destruction that, none the less, they are powerless to avoid.

When we realise these facts, and, on the other side, recall that the pressure of population is an irresistible force, and that, in the long run, no ability, no strategy, and no armament can save the castle with an insufficient garrison, then we see that the continuous existence of any civilisation that is founded upon interest is a flat impossibility.

It is astonishing to read such a work, for instance, as Mr. J. S. Mill's *Utilitarianism*, for we find therein no sign of the idea that the interests of Society and of the Race could fail to be identical. He does not point to them as separate conceptions, and there is no evidence that he

CONDEMNATION OF REASON

recognised the difference between them. Under these circumstances, it is a matter of course that he makes no reference to the possibility of any divergence in their respective interests. That this should have been so was inevitable, for the identity of their interests is a postulate—an understood premise—in any system of Utilitarianism.

Moreover, as we read that work, we feel that there was, in the mind of the writer, a frozen certitude that any form of religion was unnecessary. The question of its truth did not arise, for, in any case, it was antecedently superfluous.

Nevertheless, that which was regarded as immaterial may prove, racially, to be the one essential. Had the great utilitarians of the last century drawn the all-important distinction between Society and the Race, a different course would certainly have been taken by thought, and perhaps by history itself. For, that which it reveals is nothing less than the racial insolvency of pure Reason.

CHAPTER VIII

THE METHOD OF RELIGIOUS MOTIVE

IF, then, a civilisation resting upon a utilitarian basis is of necessity an impermanent, or, at best, an intermittent phenomenon; if, that is, the method of Reason fails racially, and so leads automatically to the disappearance of any civilisation that is founded upon it, we have next to ask: "Is every civilisation foredoomed to failure? Is the labour of building up civilisation always to prove the Sisyphean task that is disclosed in the history of all the Western civilisations of the past?"

Evidently the answer to this question involves a further consideration of what we have termed "Method." We have seen the succession of the various methods: Reflex, Instinctive, and Rational; and that, although each is an advance upon its predecessor, yet each has proved imperfect. Therefore we have to restate our question, and to ask: "Can we descry the possibility of some method that, in its turn, might supersede the method of Reason; a method disclosing new powers, and motives hitherto unconsidered, for conduct that will be of racial value?"

For a method to be entitled to take precedence of the method of Reason, it must come with great credentials.

METHOD OF RELIGIOUS MOTIVE 67

In the first place, if we are to regard it as the basis of a permanent civilisation, it must itself be permanent. It must be demonstrably free from the underlying cause of the failure that has been common to the previous methods, lest it should itself require to be superseded in the future, or liable to fail in its turn, as the methods of Instinct and Reason have failed. Thus it must be one in which the forces making for growth shall permanently overbear the forces making for decay. It must, that is, provide a basis for an ever-growing civilisation, a civilisation of ever-increasing value to the human race. It must be capable of indefinite expansion, and able to prove itself the terminus of the series of methods.

We can only see whether such a method is possible when we have exposed clearly the common and underlying cause of the incompetence that is present in all the methods that have preceded it, and not merely, as hitherto, the special manner in which this common cause has operated in each particular case. The discovery of such a common factor will furnish us with a touchstone whereby to estimate the value of any method that claims to be supra-rational, and either to accept it as genuine, or to reject it as spurious. If we find that the persistence of this factor is inevitable, then the cycle of decay will still wait upon the cycle of growth, and we shall know that a permanent civilisation is beyond the grasp of humanity.

In the second place, it must be free, more particularly, from the form of this underlying disability that we have found to be special to Reason, its immediate predecessor. This disability arises from the fact that rational conduct does not warrant the individual in subordinating his interest to that of the Race. Reason is incompetent because it provides no place for disinterested conduct.

If, then, a supra-rational method is to be competent where Reason is incompetent, it must provide, not for any enlightened self-interest, but for the voluntary self-sacrifice of the individual: a provision as unknown to the interest of rational conduct, as it is in the gratification of the impulse of pure Instinct, or the reflex response to a stimulus.

And now that we must use the word *supra-rational*, let us guard ourselves at once by pointing out that it does not carry with it any implication that Reason is discarded or even depreciated, nor that the supra-rational is either irrational or non-rational. We mean, superimposed over Reason, without the loss of anything serviceable in Reason, as Reason superseded Instinct without the loss of anything serviceable in Instinct, and as Instinct has not involved the loss of the reflexes. Civilisation cannot live by Reason alone; if it is to be stable at all, it can only be based upon the supra-rational.

Taking up now the consideration of the first of the two requirements, we ask: " What common cause of incompetence, what common element of incompleteness, is revealed in the failure of the methods of Reflex Action, Instinct, and Reason?"

In the first place, it is not quite accurate to speak of them as failures, for each has been suc-

METHOD OF RELIGIOUS MOTIVE 69

cessful in the limited area in which it was fitted to act. It will be remembered that we have already pointed out that these successive steps bear a curiously close resemblance to the steps of human scientific advance; and we may now be permitted to carry the same analogy in another direction. A scientific discovery may successfully throw light upon that which previously had baffled our comprehension. But the light has scarcely shone upon the old problem before we realise that the new discovery has itself raised a series of new problems, apparently more insoluble than the old one. Thus, as the circle of human knowledge is widened, the existence of a more and more extensive area of the unknown and mysterious is revealed beyond its circumference.

So it is with the methods or steps in the advance of civilisation. Each method has survived, because it was successful in solving the special problems that had been propounded by its predecessor. Each method has succeeded in doing so, by widening the environment of life, and bringing new powers into its service. But, with each extension of the horizon, new difficulties have sprung up—difficulties that the new method, designed to relieve those of its predecessor, is itself unable to overcome. Thus, on each occasion the environment created has proved greater than the method was fitted to deal with, and an incompleteness—a failure relative to the new environment—has resulted. We see that the power of response to an external stimulus creates, but leaves unsatisfied, the need of a power to act independently of the stimulus. The environment created by reflex power is obviously limited. The useful inborn impulses of Instinct arise and fill the gap. With the appearance of the method of Instinct the scene widens, but we have learned that the environment created by this method is, even in the impulses that are of racial value, limited to the gratification of the inborn impulses of the Individual. The environment created by inborn impulse is, then, that of the Individual. In its turn, the possession of inborn impulse has created, but left unsatisfied, the need of the power of drawing inferences. Now, in its turn, Reason fills the gap. When we reach the region of Reason, we are upon a higher eminence, and the scene is wider still. But, when our survey of the environment created by Reason is carried to its utmost limits, we find that it cannot reach beyond the interest of Society. The environment of interest is that of Society. In its turn, Reason has created, but left unsatisfied, the need of a basis of action of racial value; of action that, so far as the Individual is concerned, is purely disinterested. Thus, the common cause of inadequacy has been exposed on each occasion by a widening of the visible horizon, and the relation of Reason to its own environment has furnished no exception to this rule. The repetition of inadequacy can only be eliminated in any suprarational method if it provides us with an environment that does not admit of further extension.

Now, the broad fact that we observe, when we contemplate the general character of these several environments, is that they are limited to the earth

METHOD OF RELIGIOUS MOTIVE 71

and to earthly conditions. If we may use the word, these methods are geocentric.

Thus, a supra-rational method, if it is not to admit of further extension, must be cosmocentric: it must bring us into relation with the universe—the infinite.

If it does so, it will be demonstrably free from the common cause of inadequacy in its predecessors. Taking cognisance of the infinite, its environment would not admit of further extension. Nevertheless, within its boundary would be the possibility and promise of indefinite growth. Permanent, and of necessity the terminus of the series of methods, it would fulfil the first of our two requirements.

Next, in the presence of the infinite, do we find that the second of our two requirements, the power to make good the special disability of Reason, would be fulfilled?

Reason, taking all the earth for its province, nevertheless does but reveal the blank that separates the interest of the Race from that of Society, and the need of the self-sacrifice that alone can fill it. It recognises no guiding principle, save interest. It knows, like the Jews of old, "no king but Cæsar."

But when we are in the presence of the infinite, evidently a new position has to be taken up. Evidently a new rule of conduct has to be adopted, of conduct that is suitable to the new environment, as interested conduct is suitable to the environment of Reason. If it is to be adapted to an environment that is not earthly, it cannot be governed by earthly considerations.

On the contrary, in a life that is spent in conscious relation to the infinite, temporal interest fades into nothingness, and the significance of life is to be found only in its relation to the infinite.

And the meaning of the life that is significant in the presence of the infinite is expressed in service. And the life of significant service is a life of reasoned self-sacrifice.

Thus, a supra-rational method, bringing with it the power of self-sacrifice, shows itself to be free from the limitations that made Reason incompetent, and fulfils the second of our two requirements.

If, for the purpose of these pages, we may define religion as conscious relation to the infinite, and recognise in service the expression of that conscious relation, what else is this service than a method of religious motive? Henceforward we shall speak, not of a supra-rational method, but of a method of Religious Motive.

We have already seen that the general stress of life consists of two constant elements: the social, or competitive stress, and the racial, or reproductive stress. We have already examined their incidence; first, under inborn impulse, the method of Instinct; and then under interest, the method of Reason. We have tried these methods, and found them wanting in the power to deal adequately with one or the other stress. Under the method of Instinct we found inability to deal with the competitive or social stress, for it involved a limitless waste of individual lives. Under the method of Reason we found inability to deal with the reproductive or

METHOD OF RELIGIOUS MOTIVE

racial stress, on account of the necessary disappearance of any civilisation based upon interest.

And now, if we would test the value of Religion as the basis of civilisation, we must pass on to the examination of the reception of these two stresses under the method of Religious Motive. There we shall find ourselves in a new world of thought, and under a wider sky, where the appearance of considerations that are of infinite significance leads to the surrender of those that are temporal; where the deliberate and frank self-sacrifice of the Individual is available, and duty takes the place of interest.

CHAPTER IX

THE RELATION OF THE METHOD OF RELIGIOUS MOTIVE TO THE SOCIAL STRESS: THE DUTY OF THE INDIVIDUAL WITH REGARD TO SOCIETY

"But one conclusion he (the Scientific Historical Inquirer) may properly draw from the facts bearing upon the subject before us. Nobody is at liberty to attack several property and to say at the same time that he values civilisation. The history of the two cannot be disentangled. Civilisation is nothing more than a name for the old order of the Aryan world, dissolved, but perpetually reconstituting itself under a vast variety of solvent influences, of which infinitely the most powerful have been those which have, slowly, and in some parts of the world much less perfectly than in others, substituted several property for collective ownership."[1]

THE method of Religious Motive is so wholly distinct from its predecessors, the difference in perspective caused by the change from geocentric to cosmocentric conduct is so vast, that before it is possible to undertake the examination of its own sufficiency as the basis of a permanent civilisation by testing the manner of its working in relation to the two great permanent stresses, it is necessary to examine the method itself in greater detail.

Once more we see a new method dominated by a new idea and making an entirely fresh departure. The method of Religious Motive, in contrast with the method of Instinct and the

[1] Sir Henry Maine, *Village Communities*, p. 230, third edition, 1876.

RELIGION AND SOCIETY

method of Reason, is, by its very nature, dependent on the real existence of the cosmocentric significance of conduct.

The fatalist, holding that the future has been foreordained and rendered as unchangeable as the past, believes that all things, himself included, are controlled in their course by a power that acts *ab extra*. Thus he cannot be said to recognise that his conduct is of either geocentric or cosmocentric import. The determinist, holding that the future has not been thus petrified by an external fiat, nevertheless believes that all things, himself included, are wholly conditioned by the immutable past, and controlled *ab intra*. He recognises that, just as he is the creature of his own past life and of the antecedents from which he sprang, so, in his turn, he is the antecedent of the consequences that flow from his acts. Accordingly he seeks to follow the line of enlightened conduct that is expedient in its consequences, and, to him, conduct is purely of geocentric import.

But the lifelong self-sacrifice of a rational being cannot be justified on rational grounds. Here no geocentric motive will avail. A rule of conduct that takes temporal things as an end will not suffice: a religion *ad hoc* will not serve. If the Freedom of the Will is not in our possession, then, *cadit quaestio*. For then it is evident that humanity is circumscribed by pure Reason, and limited to a method that has already been discussed, and dismissed as incapable of furnishing the basis of a permanent civilisation.

If, on the contrary, that Freedom be indeed

in our possession, then, and then only, is conduct invested with the dignity of cosmocentric significance, and ruled by a conscious relation to the infinite. That relation, and that relation alone, brings with it the supra-rational motive that creates and inspires a sense of cosmocentric duty, and provides a valid justification for the voluntary and lifelong self-sacrifice of a rational being. In that relation is a rule of conduct that is not *ad hoc*, a Religion that comes with its own authority—an authority external to ourselves—and with an imperative power that is inherent in itself. It brings with it behests that stand above the demands of the Race, and that are higher than the claims of Society. For, in the method of cosmocentric motive, the cosmocentric significance of conduct is everything. When we think of the overwhelming importance of the "*vraie signification de la vie*," no other consideration weighs even as dust in the balance. Earthly conduct, whether concerning the Race or Society, being no longer an end, has become an instrument. The end is no longer temporal, although we deal with temporality. The unselfish conduct that serves the Race, or benefits Society, becomes no more than the means of expressing the consciousness of our relation to the infinite; the means of conferring cosmocentric significance upon the brief life of the individual, and creating a bond with the eternal.

This, then, is the method whose efficiency we have now to estimate, testing it, as we tested the method of Instinct and the method of Reason, by the evidence that it can bring forward of ability

RELIGION AND SOCIETY 77

to deal successfully with the two great permanent stresses of life. In the case of each stress we have first to inquire what course the method will seek to take; and then to ask whether it has the power to take that course. First we address ourselves to the social stress, and, just as in considering the relations of Reason with the social stress, we asked firstly: "Is it to the interest of the individual to abolish competition?" and secondly: "Is it in his power to do so?" So now we ask firstly: "Is it the duty of the Individual to accept a competitive life?" or, in the alternative; "Is it his duty to adopt a non-competitive life?" and secondly we ask: "Is this duty one that it is in his power to carry out? Is it in his power, that is, in the light of the life significant?"

We have, then, to begin by asking whether it is the duty of the Individual to perpetuate the conditions of unlimited strife? The question carries the answer upon the face of it. The adoption of unlimited competition would result in a reversion to the moral surroundings of the already socially-discredited method of Instinct. That, as we saw, is a method of inconceivable wastefulness and ruthlessness, knowing, at its best, no more than the self-sacrifice of inborn impulse. In effect, it is a world of self-seeking, where such a thing as supra-rational self-sacrifice is all unknown. No system could be more distantly removed from the life of significance. From the standpoint of religious motive, the self-seeking of unlimited competition is not socially a-moral, it is actively immoral, for it knows no moral law. The Competitive Method, and the Method of Religious Motive, are the very antitheses of one another, and the adoption of the former involves the failure of the latter.

Next, then, we have to consider what would be the moral position of the Individual in the absence of competition, and amid the surroundings of the racially-discredited method of Reason. The racial aspect of the matter will be discussed in the next chapter. At present we have only to consider the moral position of an Individual in a world wherein all property would be vested in Society, and nothing could be owned by the Individual.

Such a system of life may be, speciously but falsely, represented as though it were altruistic. It is easy to paint the alluring picture of a world that knows nothing of the warfare that we have called the social, or competitive stress; of a millennium wherein each one is indirectly seeking the good of all, while all are indirectly seeking the good of each. This view has been expressed in the well-known phrase: "Each for all, and all for each."

But—herein is no true altruism.

Deprived of the power of working for his private advantage, every member of Society would be interested in raising the general standard of living, in order himself to share in the improved conditions. To take this course would be merely the behaviour of a rational person. There would be no unselfish element in his direct motive. It is still purely a matter of interest. It is also inevitably a matter of interest. One member of a

RELIGION AND SOCIETY 79

Socialistic Society can only benefit another indirectly, and by advancing the common good. But this advance is to his own interest; therein he also shares. Deprived of the power of working for his private advantage, he is also deprived of the power of seeking the good of his contemporaries by the sacrifice of his private interest. In the same manner, action that is injurious to his contemporaries, that is, to the social machine, is merely the behaviour of a fool. It injures the doer as much as any of his fellows. The avoidance of such conduct is also necessarily interested. The geocentric motive follows conduct into its minutest ramifications; it cannot be shaken off. The member of a Socialist Society may have every advantage of freedom from anxiety, of material welfare, and æsthetic enjoyment. He has gained the whole world, but he has sold his soul. Small wonder that, as we pointed out in Chap. V, horror is inspired by such a life, intense in proportion to the nakedness with which its rational character is exposed. Small wonder that, in its advocacy, pure Reason loses its old-time cogency especially and essentially among the least selfish members of the community—among those, that is, to whom the significance of life is life itself; those to whom the consciousness of relation with the infinite comes with its own authority. Let us make no mistake. Competition, indeed, is abolished. But if the self-seeking of competition disappears, so also does every possibility of unselfish conduct. To such an order the word "moral" does not apply.

The converse is also true.

Such a system of life might, also with speciousness and falsity, be represented as though it were selfish. A repulsive picture of it may be painted as easily as an alluring one—the picture of a world in which no individual directly sought the good of Society, and in which no one directly sought to benefit him. In point of fact, a non-competitive world might be described by the phrase "None for all, and all for no one," quite as accurately as by the phrase that we have quoted above. It is only that we are looking at the reverse side of the medal, instead of the obverse.

But—there is herein no true selfishness.

Interested in raising the general standard of living, in order to share in the improved conditions, every member of a Socialistic Society would nevertheless be deprived of the power of working directly for his own private advantage. For it is evident that, as a common ownership, with the one hand, takes away all possibility of unselfish action, so, with the other hand, it takes away all possibility of self-seeking at the expense of contemporaries. Theoretically, such a system has eliminated all selfish promptings, and, under it, when a man shapes his life merely to his own advantage, there can be no directly selfish element in the mode by which he seeks this end.

To such an order the word "immoral" does not apply.

Individual conduct, under a socialistic form of Society, is then, of necessity, neither moral nor immoral; it is as blankly a-moral as pure Reason

RELIGION AND SOCIETY

itself, whose legitimate offspring it is. When life has been denuded of all competitive environment, it has also been emptied of all moral content, and we find that, in the method of Religious Motive, hostility to a non-competitive life is *articulus stantis aut cadentis*.

Thus the method of Religious Motive would be equally stultified by the adoption, either of a system of unlimited competition, or of a purely non-competitive system. A deadlock appears to have been reached, and the second question arises: " Is it, after all, within the power of the individual to avoid, at the same time, the socially immoral character of the competitive method of Instinct, and the socially a-moral character of the non-competitive method of Reason? Is it within his power so to frame his life, that his social conduct shall be of cosmocentric significance?"

In answering this question, it must be borne in mind that two elements are necessary for significance in conduct. The first is liberty. Now, in our use of the word "liberty" there will be no reference to freedom of will. It will be used only with reference to external circumstances that are of such a nature as may either provide opportunity for the exercise of that freedom, or render its possession nugatory and valueless. The man, whose external circumstances are those of a prison, has little opportunity for its exercise, as compared with the man on horseback. Such liberty—the opportunity of acting in a manner that may be moral or immoral—is lost under the socially a-moral method of Reason. For, thereunder a man is deprived both of the opportunity of working directly for his own private advantage, and of directly seeking the good of his contemporaries by its sacrifice.

The second element that is necessary for significance in conduct is law, and the opportunity of acting in a manner that, by the surrender of liberty, makes service truly significant—an opportunity that is lost in the social chaos of the method of Instinct. It will be observed that the area within which significant conduct is possible extends as far, and only as far, as we have both liberty and law simultaneously.

How, then, can competition help? Has it anything to offer when we seek these essentials? We see clearly that it has, that the competitive method furnishes liberty to the individual, and that it only fails to be significant socially, because it excludes all moral law.

How can the method of Reason help? We see that, as against the social chaos of Instinct, it stands for law, and that it fails to be significant socially, only because it excludes all moral liberty.

A remarkable situation is thus disclosed.

Each method fails to confer significance upon conduct when it is carried out alone, and yet, if each were limited by the other, the two together —the competitive and the non-competitive— would succeed. Each would furnish one of the two elements that are necessary antecedents to significance in conduct. If, that is, each could be taken as the complement of the other, if the one could come into operation at the point at which the other would become destructive if it stood alone, then the reciprocating machinery of a method of Religious Motive would have been put together ready to act as a whole.

But, as we have already pointed out (page 59), they cannot amalgamate spontaneously. They possess no power to do so. Pure Reason, the enemy of the Race, knows only the interest of the Individual, or rather, of Society. Instinct, on the other hand, is the servant of the Race, and the enemy of Society. The history of the growth of Reason is the history of the overthrow of Instinct. Prepotent Reason excludes the office of Instinct, and, if they were alone, the prepotence would be temporary; having obtained the mastery, it would become self-destructive, and Instinct would come by its own again. The hostility is essential; they are mutually exclusive.

Therefore the conditions have changed, and we see that the answer to the question that we are discussing, viz.: " Is it within the power of the Individual so to frame his life that his conduct shall be of cosmocentric significance?" depends upon the answer to the narrower and antecedent question: " Is it within his power to use each method to make good the flaw in the other? Does he, that is, possess a solvent of each, a power over both, that shall enable them to enter into combination?"

It will be remembered that, at the beginning of this chapter, we saw that the method of Religious Motive was possessed of a quality that distinguished it from its predecessors, and that we found this distinctive quality in the fact that it comes with an authority external to ourselves. In order that this distinctive quality may be thrown into greater relief, let us approach the question by comparing the geocentric methods, from which it is absent. Take the method of Reason: the purely rational being is both servant and master, for he serves himself. His allegiance is to himself; the care of himself is his work. His allegiance is, then, to his work. In this work a non-competitive system is his instrument. But, just as he is at once his own servant and his own master, so his instrument and his work are one. He cannot vary, that is, from his non-competitive system, for then, as we have seen, it would become inevitable that he should injure himself. He possesses no selective power. He is chained to the oar, as much as the instinctive animal is chained to the foregone conclusions of inborn impulse.

But these conditions do not obtain at all in the method of Religious Motive; they are obviated by the distinctive quality of that method—by the fact that it comes with its own authority, and with an imperative power that is inherent in itself. The Individual becomes a servant only; his allegiance is not to himself, but to him whom he serves; a life of significant service is his work, and competition and its reverse are alike no more than his instruments. He is a servant; his allegiance is not primarily to his work, and not at all to his instruments. He is not chained to them, he possesses the power of selection; he may lay down

RELIGION AND SOCIETY 85

one, and take up another, as suits the purpose of the work before him. He may lay down a competitive system and take up a non-competitive one, or vice versa, as the significance of his life demands.

Thus we find that the method of Religious Motive is able to retain the element that is of value to the significance of life in each geocentric system, and at the same time able to reject the social a-morality of the one, and the social immorality of the other.

So far as Society is concerned, it retains the element of liberty, necessary to significance in social conduct, that belongs to the method of Instinct, and so obviates the social a-morality of Reason. At the same time, it retains the element of law, not less essential than liberty to significance in social conduct, that belongs to the method of Reason. The liberty of the competitive system, thus conditioned by the law of the non-competitive method, becomes the liberty of a trustee. Does a man win in the contest? The prize does not belong to him, except in name: he is a trustee. Under the law, all that he gains by competition he must forego in a manner that is the very negation of self-seeking. Does he lose in the contest? Provision for his needs becomes the object of the trust. Thus the internal friction of the social machine is reduced to a minimum, and the retention of the element of law, that belongs to the method of Reason—the subjection, that is, of the Individual to Society—obviates the social immorality of the method of Instinct.

It will be seen, moreover, that, in the method of Religious Motive, it is the Individual himself who takes his own course. For if, on the one hand, his action is forcibly controlled—if his liberty is taken away by external circumstances—so also is the significance of his conduct removed. And if, on the other hand, his action has not the opportunity of being controlled by a law that he ought to obey—if such a law is not provided by external circumstances—then again, the significance of his conduct is removed. To be significant, his action must be from within. Constrained conduct, like lawless conduct, however right, is not righteous. The strained mercy, twice damned—that takes away the grace of life and curses the giver with the sense of state-compulsion, and curses the recipient with the sense of booty acquired—is alien to the cosmocentric method. In that method, and in that only, is the grace of life to be found—the grace that blesses the giver and the taker, the grace that binds together. And he who will can trace herein the injunction that comes to us from of old, that we should love one another.

The conclusion reached is, then, that the cosmocentric method, possessed of the power to retain both liberty and law, provides a machinery for significant conduct that is perfect, so far as Society is concerned. The duty of the Individual, with regard to competition, and with regard to non-competition, has become clear, and the power of the method of Religious Motive to deal successfully with the social stress stands vindicated.

CHAPTER X

THE RELATION OF THE METHOD OF RELIGIOUS MOTIVE TO THE RACIAL STRESS: THE DUTY OF THE INDIVIDUAL WITH REGARD TO THE RACE

OUR next step is to ask what evidence the method of Religious Motive brings forward of ability to cope with the racial stress. We must estimate its racial efficiency by applying the now familiar test of inquiring, firstly, what course it will seek to take, and, secondly, whether it has the power to take that course.

First, then, we seek to know the duty that, as an element in the life of significance, the Individual owes to the Race. We ask, that is: "Is it the duty of the Individual to carry the multiplication of the Race to its utmost limits, as is done in the method of Instinct?" or, in the alternative: "Is it his duty to act in a contrary manner, as would be done in the method of Reason?"

Having arrived at an answer to these questions, we then ask: "Is this duty one that is in his power, consistently with the cosmocentric significance of life, to carry out? Is it within the power of the Individual so to frame his life that his racial conduct shall be of cosmocentric significance?"

What we have called the social immorality of the method of Instinct already stands condemned. Its racial morality is now in question. The method of Instinct makes provision for the due perpetuation of the Race—it sacrifices the Individual without mercy in the pursuit of that aim. It cannot be said that such a system is racially immoral. Nevertheless, it knows no liberty in the matter—it knows not the liberty to regulate the birthrate that is given by Reason, and thus, for lack of this liberty, it cannot, from the point of view of the method of Religious Motive, be said to have any moral quality. It makes due provision for the perpetuation of the Race: it is not racially immoral. In the pursuit of this aim, however, it knows no liberty: it is not racially moral. Judged by the standard of cosmocentric motive, the method of Instinct, socially immoral, is found to be racially a-moral, because it knows no racial liberty.

We have next to consider the moral aspect of the alternative method of Reason, a method already racially discredited as one that, cutting off the entail of life, would spend its riches upon Society. But, what is morally involved in such conduct? When we consider the æons of the future, and the generations that are, perhaps, to come, we not only see that the question is one of life or no-life, upon a stupendous, indeed upon a measureless scale, but also that the lives that are, perhaps, to follow after us, are lives of significance. In the provision or non-provision, of life for the days to come, it is the provision, or non-provision, of significance itself that is really at stake. If we default now, that which is lacking will not be made good. So far as we can see, the very existence of significance, throughout a measureless future, depends upon our acts in the present. So far as we can see, we stand before One Who gathers where He has not strawed; Who, in the faithful discharge of our duties to Society, sees no more than the return of the one talent that was handed to us. Thus the continuance of the entail is an essential part of the inheritance, vital to the method of Religious Motive, and it is the very height of lawlessness, by failing in the obligation that came with the inheritance, to secure the destruction of entailed significance at the wanton bidding of Reason. Judged by the cosmocentric standard, the method of Reason, socially a-moral, is found to be racially immoral, because it knows no racial law.

Thus the method of Religious Motive would be equally stultified by the exclusive adoption of the racial element in either of the geocentric methods: it is precluded from doing so by the racial a-morality of Instinct, and the racial immorality of Reason. So far as racial conduct is concerned, they are alike destructive to the significance of life, and again a deadlock appears to have been reached analogous to that encountered when, in the last chapter (page 78), we were dealing with the social aspect of the question.

Thus the second question arises: " Is it within the power of the Individual to avoid, at the same time, the racially a-moral character of the method of Instinct, and the racially immoral character of the method of Reason? Is it within his power so to frame his life that his conduct, with regard to the Race, shall be of cosmocentric significance?"

The analogy of the present argument, dealing with the Race, with that in the last chapter, dealing with Society, is now becoming evident, and it may, perhaps, be seen most clearly by a diagrammatic summary of the geocentric systems, as they appear from the point of view of the method of Religious Motive.

		Society	Race
Instinct		Society sacrificed for the sake of the Race. Social liberty, but no social law. Socially immoral. No significance owing to absence of law.	Devoted to service of Race. Racial law, but no racial liberty. Racially a-moral. No significance owing to absence of liberty.
Reason		Devoted to service of Society. Social law, but no social liberty. Socially a-moral. No significance owing to absence of liberty.	Race sacrificed for the sake of Society. Racial liberty, but no racial law. Racially immoral. No significance owing to absence of law.

Recalling (page 81) that the area within which significant conduct is possible extends so far, and only so far, as we have at the same time both liberty and law, we ask whether these geocentric systems

RELIGION AND THE RACE

have anything to offer racially, when we seek for these essentials.

We find that they have. We see that, as against the racial destructiveness—the anarchy—that is involved in the method of Reason, Instinct furnishes law, and that it only fails to be significant racially, because it cannot vary its method; it excludes liberty. In the like manner, we see that Reason has provided us with racial liberty—the power of controlling the birthrate—and that it only fails to be significant because it knows no racial law.

Thus when either stands alone, it fails to confer racial significance upon conduct, and yet, if each were limited by the other, the two together would succeed. If, that is, each were to be taken as the complement of the other, if each could come into operation at the point at which the other would become non-significant if it stood alone, then racial conduct would have become significant.

But, by themselves, this is impossible. We have already seen that they are mutually exclusive, and that they cannot amalgamate spontaneously. Therefore the answer to the question that we are discussing, viz.: " Is it within the power of the Individual so to frame his life that his racial conduct shall be of cosmocentric significance?" turns upon the answer to the narrower and antecedent question: " Is it within his power to use the advantage of each method—the law of the one and the liberty of the other—and to shun, at the same time, their respective disadvantages?"

Again, we find such a power in the method of Religious Motive. That method comes with external authority. Under its imperative influence the individual is not bound by either of the geocentric methods; they become no more than instruments in his hands.

The law under which he has himself come into the possession of life—the law that justifies his own existence—is the law of entail. He inherited owing to the operation of that law. If his own life is to be significant, he must remember that the law is definite. The entail must not be selfishly broken.

But liberty—the power that Reason gives to break the entail—is not less essential to significance than is the law itself. Only in the presence of that power can obedience to the law become a significant act.

Thus we find that the selective power of the method of Religious Motive enables it to retain all that is of value to significance in each of the geocentric methods. So far as the Race is concerned, it retains the law—the subjection of the Individual to the Race—that is characteristic of the method of Instinct, and thus obviates the racial destructiveness that is characteristic of Reason. It retains, at the same time, the racial liberty that comes with Reason, and thus obviates the racial a-morality of Instinct.

The cosmocentric importance of the racial duty of the individual is now clear. The method of Religious Motive, retaining both law and liberty, both service and freedom, provides a perfect machinery for significance in racial conduct, and its power to deal with the racial stress, no less successfully than with the social stress, stands vindicated.

CHAPTER XI

MUTUAL RELATIONS OF SOCIETY AND THE RACE UNDER THE METHOD OF RELIGIOUS MOTIVE

IN order to complete our review of the mutual dependence of the members of the triad that we are considering—the Individual, Society, and the Race—the relations of the two latter claim our attention next. Seeing that the unborn Race cannot, of itself, take part in this interaction, our inquiry is narrowed down to the consideration of the position that Society, moved by a sense of cosmocentric duty, will take up towards the Race. Strictly speaking, it is, of course, impossible to regard Society as possessed of duties in the same manner as an individual, for the duty of Society, if we may make use of the phrase, is no more than the duty of individuals acting in concert. Nevertheless, it is natural that the corporate action of a number of individuals, prompted by the influence of Religious Motive, should be very different from the action that they would take under the influence of pure Reason.

It will be remembered that, when we reached a parallel position in dealing with the action of Society under the method of Reason, we found that its interest was identical with that of the Individual, and its attitude towards the Race not

RELIGIOUS SOCIETY AND RACE

less hostile. But we have seen already that this attitude of the Individual towards the Race is reversed in the method of Religious Motive, and that cosmocentric considerations require him to act unselfishly, and in favour of the Race.

Therefore, when we pass from the method of Reason and interest to that of Religious Motive and duty, the action of Society will be reversed also; it also will become ancillary to the Race, for racial duty will not be less binding when Individuals act in social concert.

The question then arises: " In what manner will this new attitude of Society manifest itself?" In seeking the answer to this question, we must hark back to the cause of the hostility of Society to the Race under the method of Reason. It will be remembered that we found this ultimately in the inequality of the length of life between the transitory Society (a length on the average the same as that of the Individual) and the longevous Race. It is necessary to recall this, because, although the method of Religious Motive is not directly concerned with geocentric interests or their reconciliation, we find that the said inequality nevertheless introduces a new problem into that method. The dim future of the Race is far removed from the purview of the Individual, and the manner, therefore, in which he can carry out his duty, to those so distant from him, is obscure and uncertain.

Thus it comes about that, without consideration for the individual's interest, the racial duty of individuals acting in concert—of Society, that is—is confined to the provision of the means whereby that duty will be set clearly before its members.

This is the very office of Society acting racially under the method of Religious Motive. All its organisation, so far as it conforms racially to that method, will be tributary to the provision of definite means whereby the Individual can serve the Race; to the forging of a link that shall join the living of the present to the living of the future.

We find that Society has provided this link in the organisation of the family as a social institution.

The life of the family, longer than that of the Individual, shorter than that of the Race, is not incommensurable with either. In the institution of the family, we can trace the nexus that Society, acting under the influence of the method that we are considering, has created between the two. The duty of the Individual with regard to the long-drawn life of the Race, otherwise so dim and uncertain, becomes clear-cut and definite when it is transmuted into duty to the family from which he springs, whose love he shares, whose traditions he inherits, and whose name he must hand on. We have seen (page 52) that marriage would be the height of folly in a purely rational Individual, and (page 58) that any equivalent maintenance of the Race would not be less irrational in a communist Society. We see now, however, under the method of Religious Motive, that marriage becomes the very means for the performance of the racial duty of the Individual. Married, he becomes one of those who are consecrated for the provision of

RELIGIOUS SOCIETY AND RACE 97

significance itself in the future, and the water of his life is turned into wine.

Thus the maintenance of the institution of the family stands in relation to Society much as the duty of significant racial conduct stands to the Individual.

Small wonder, then, that the family should, among so many and such various peoples, and in ages so far removed from one another, have been regarded with veneration as an institution possessed of a semi-sacred character, and as one connected with the expression of the religious sense of a community. This sentiment extends even beyond the limits of any particular formation of the family. Among ourselves, the home is inviolable, and the marriage that has not received the sanction of religion is regarded with doubt and contempt. Among Mohammedans, the Nazarene can live and carry on daily intercourse cheerfully, but only on condition that he recollects that there are two subjects to which he must never refer—the Mohammedan's God, and the Mohammedan's women. Among the Chinese, as we shall see further on, sentiment regards the connection between the family and the faith as even more intimate. In the mind of the Chinaman they are indissoluble; they have been fused into one conception and are identified with one another.

It is also interesting to observe that the occasions of the public expression of the emotions are frequently found in events connected with the family. The widespread hospitality of the festivities of a wedding, the congratulations that attend upon the birth of a child, and the mourning that is openly worn by the relatives when death has visited their number, are all acknowledgments that the family possesses an importance that extends beyond its threshold. Love of home, again, is closely connected with love of country, and the conception that Society is the protector of the family is expressed in patriotism.

If we recall once more the fact that, in the method of Reason, the respective interests of Society and the Race are diametrically opposed to one another, it becomes evident that the family —the nexus by which Society, under the influence of Religious Motive, has joined the two—is an institution that is not to be justified in pure Reason. Thus, when Society, acting in its own interest, forgets that its racial duty is focussed upon the family, the evils that follow are necessarily racial in character. The operation of the English death duties may be taken as an example. These constitute a frontal attack upon the family as an institution. The legislation that is responsible for them regards the death of a father as an opportunity for plundering his children, and Society reaps the benefit. Looking at the matter, however, from a racial point of view, we see that, short of actually fining a man for the possession of offspring, it would be difficult to conceive a more direct incitement to the commission of racial suicide by what is termed "limitation of the family."

The corporate action of Society with regard to the future is largely determined by voting, and

RELIGIOUS SOCIETY AND RACE 99

such legislation as the above will continue so long as the family is ignored in the polling-booth, and the childless of either sex—those, that is, who have social, but no racial duties—are admitted to the franchise on equal terms with the parents of legitimate children. Properly, the franchise is an appurtenance of the family and not of the individual. The qualification for it should be the possession of legitimate children; and its exercise should be the joint act of two parents, or the sole act of the survivor of them. The character of Society in the present day is disclosed by the fact that one might as well cry for the moon as ask for the realisation of these views. Nevertheless, it will only be when they have been realised that there will be an end of the time-serving that is the bane of representative government and the curse of democracy. Indeed, if we would know the worth of any form of government, of any policy, or of any legislation, let us ask whether, or no, it tends to strengthen the family, and to advance the honour of the married state. This is the supreme test of social action, and the very criterion of statesmanship. For, if the family is not the unit of Society, nor the unit of the Race, but the nexus between the two, then the honour and importance that are attached to it, and the rigidity with which it is maintained, will give us a measure of the vitality of any civilisation.

CHAPTER XII

JUSTIFICATION OF THE METHOD OF RELIGIOUS MOTIVE

WHETHER we look at past history, or the prevailing condition of modern life, we see that the authority of cosmocentric motive, though it has ebbed and flowed, has not been, and is not yet, the dominant influence in the civilisation of the white man. It has not been successful on a great scale in that civilisation in the past. The history of Europe, in spite of the nominal sway of a wholly cosmocentric religion for more than a thousand years, records great nations and cultures that have declined and practically disappeared. If we turn to the present, we find that the authority of cosmocentric motive is a decaying force. Day by day we see the increasing revolt against both the social and the racial stress. We see the ever-rising prominence of views that, whether they bear the label of Socialism or not, are socialistic in character, and also an ever-falling birthrate that, from year to year, is the "lowest on record." These phenomena are not confined to one nation or tongue; they are practically co-extensive with all Western civilisation. Are we then to say that the method of Religious Motive has failed ?

Certainly not. When disasters occur, it is

METHOD OF RELIGIOUS MOTIVE

unreasonable to blame the seer whose warnings were disregarded, or the leader whose directions were disobeyed. That which counsels endurance of the two stresses should not be held responsible when revolt takes place. Recorded history, as we have said before, is a complex resultant of forces, and we are only concerned with the directions in which its invisible components act. Our argument is not affected by their relative magnitudes. The past and present facts of European history do no more than show that the method of Reason is still dominant, and that the liability to fail, no less than the possibility of success, is implicit in the liberty that is demanded by the method of Religious Motive.

But little remains. In the preceding chapters we have seen that the method of Religious Motive does not seek geocentric interest, but cosmocentric significance; that it involves therefore endurance of both social and racial stress; but that, in each case, it does so under its own conditions, and with its own limitations. In neither case is the burden shouldered for its own sake, but only as the means whereby to lead a life of cosmocentric significance; in the one case, as a means of significance in social conduct, and in the other, as a means of significance in racial conduct. Thus we have seen that true action in regard to the social stress is that of the trustee. The life of competition is, indeed, adopted, but that which is gained as a result of competitive effort is only a fund to be administered in a manner that is the very negation of self-seeking. The law is maintained; but, so far as Society is concerned, it is limited by liberty.

The same is true of the racial stress. The estate of life is entailed, and we found that the law enjoins that the entail should not be selfishly broken by the life-tenant, and yet that circumstances are imaginable in which it might become a legacy of evil, and that an unselfish liberty would then take the place of law. The principle may be illustrated by a strange quotation from the Gospel according to the Egyptians. The passage is referred to several times by Clement of Alexandria, and runs thus: " When Salome asked how long death would prevail, the Lord said: 'So long as ye women bear children. For I have come to destroy the works of the female.' And Salome said to him: 'Did I therefore well in bearing no children?' The Lord answered, and said: 'Eat every herb, but eat not that which hath bitterness.'" The last words raise Salome's second question into the region of significance—of conduct that is right or wrong. If we are free to eat of every herb, except "that which hath bitterness," we see that the answer implies liberty as well as law.

This conjunction is the very note of the method of Religious Motive, a method within which, though there is service, yet there is perfect freedom: the co-ordination of law and liberty, a co-ordination that, within the confines of Reason, many have sought and none have found.

Thus we see that both Society and the Race are guarded—the importance of each is recognised.

METHOD OF RELIGIOUS MOTIVE 103

The method of Religious Motive, falling neither into the racial immorality and social a-morality of Reason, nor into the racial a-morality and social immorality of Instinct, avoids both Scylla and Charybdis.

And the Individual: what of him? In the "Valley of Decision" he bears the burden of both, and duty is his portion. But for what else can he ask than for this? He does not measure by a geocentric standard: the method that judges by interest is far removed from him. He measures by quite another standard—the standard of cosmocentric significance. And, in the method of Religious Motive he finds all that he needs, a machinery that is perfect, both socially and racially, for the voluntary and lifelong self-sacrifice of a rational being; the only one that is capable of furnishing a true and stable civilisation.

Geocentric action seeks a permanent civilisation as an end, but cannot attain it. Cosmocentric action attains it, but does not seek it as an end. A permanent civilisation may indeed come, but can only do so as an accident of self-sacrifice that is offered upon the altars of the Most High.

PART II

HISTORICAL ILLUSTRATION OF THE PRINCIPLES INDICATED IN THE PRECEDING CHAPTERS

CHAPTER I

ROME AND CHINA

WE have had such frequent occasion to point out that history is a resultant from which it is impossible to determine either the direction or magnitude of its components that, at first sight, it seems absurd that we should turn to the examination of the records of past or present civilisations. But to take that view would be to misunderstand our present purpose. Although the components cannot be divined from a given resultant, the reverse process is perfectly possible. If the magnitude of the components and their directions are known, then their effect can be traced in the resultant. It is this reversed course that we propose to take. We shall assume that in the preceding pages we have discovered the components of history, and we now propose, first to identify them in the records of the past, and then to trace their effect. Such an application of the general principles that we have reached is not only legitimate, but necessary, for it furnishes the only possible means whereby their truth can be tested. We shall, though we do not intend to confine ourselves to them exclusively, investigate two great examples of civilisation. Each of them is typical, and they stand in striking contrast to one another. The first will exemplify the preponderance of the forces that we have indicated as making for decay. In this instance, we must be able to show that, founded on Reason, it was a geocentric civilisation, and that its religions were strictly what we have called *ad hoc*, that they were subservient to the State and part of its polity. We must then be able to show the process of revolt against the two primary stresses; the appearance of socialistic phenomena, accompanied by the assumption of supreme and intrusive power by the State, and the appearance and prevalence of race-suicide, followed by the gradual collapse of the huge structure.

The other civilisation will exemplify the preponderance of the forces that we have indicated as making for permanence and continuous growth. Here we must be able to demonstrate that the prevailing religion is strictly cosmocentric, that the resulting civilisation is supra-rational in character; that is to say, that it has been, and is, marked by submission to each of the two primary stresses. Socially, we must find a stoical endurance of the competition of life carried on at its maximum of severity. The resulting social conditions may present a picture that is repellent to ourselves, and we may find that the individual life is of little account. We shall expect to see that the religious sanctions of the family have given it so great an importance that it has displaced and well-nigh obliterated the idea of the State; that patriotism is almost unknown, and that the State

ROME AND CHINA

only exists so far as is indispensable to the safety of the family. We must be able to show that, springing from the religious veneration of the family, submission to the racial stress is not less in evidence. We may find, indeed, that this is the cause of the harshness of the social conditions. If such a civilisation has already persisted for a long time, we must be able to show that it is shared by multitudes innumerable. We must be able to show that, however ancient it may be, it is still in the ascendant, and that its zenith is incalculable.

If we find that the former, the geocentric civilisation, in spite of the social splendour of the day of its greatness, has gradually collapsed in disaster; and that the latter, the cosmocentric civilisation, in spite of the severity of its social conditions, is still flourishing racially, and that, in spite of its antiquity, it is still at the dawn of its history, then we may justly claim that our conclusions have been tested and found true.

About the beginning of the Christian Era the world — speaking roughly and not minutely — possessed two great civilisations. Although contemporaries, each was little more than cognisant of the fact that the other existed, for they were so widely separated geographically that they scarcely came into contact with one another. One was the Roman civilisation, the other the Chinese. Their contact, one of the most arresting episodes in history, is recorded by Chinese historians. They relate that in the ninth year of Yau-hi (A.D. 166) an embassy, which appears to have come by sea, arrived in their country from Ta-thsin, sent by An-thun, or Marcus Aurelius Antoninus. Unfortunately we do not often bear in mind the fact that these empires were not only contemporaries, but that the Chinese civilisation arose at a time long anterior to that of Rome, and was coeval with the Pharaohs.

The one race has disappeared: the other remains; and not only remains, but in the minds of those who know it, constitutes the most tremendous factor in the world of to-day. Why has the one disappeared? And, still more, why is the other, the most ancient, still the youngest of the nations?

To find the answers to these questions will be the main object of our historical investigations, although we must not lose sight of other examples that are not less instructive. Why has the Athenian vanished? Why is the Jew indestructible?

CHAPTER II

RELIGION UNDER THE ROMAN EMPIRE

AT the time of the assassination of Julius Cæsar the Roman Republic had attained the "dissolute greatness" that marked its later years, but it was unequal to the administration of the whole Western world, and already the omens portended its fall. After the death of Cæsar the State was convulsed for thirteen years by a succession of civil wars, and at the end of that period, Augustus, the first and greatest of the emperors, was supreme and his authority unquestioned. "He knitted together the Roman world,[1] east and west, into one great organisation, of which the emperor stood as the supreme head. He set his legions upon the distant frontiers, and their swords formed a wall of steel within which commerce and peace might flourish. The security was not perpetual, yet it lasted for four centuries, and saved ancient civilisation from destruction. . . . The seeds of degeneration and decay had been planted in the days of the Republic, and would have come to maturity far sooner if there had been no Augustus and no empire. Augustus started the Roman world on a new career."

[1] *Augustus Cæsar and the Organisation of the Empire of Rome*, pp. 364 *et seq.* By John B. Firth, B.A. G. P. Putnam's Sons, 1903.

112   THE FATE OF EMPIRES

The history of the temporary renascence that was achieved by Augustus, and of the fate that overtook it, is most instructive for our present purpose, for it shows us the deliberate and conscious effort of a man of genius, ruling the world, not only to arrest the decadence, but to establish a permanent civilisation. The magnitude of the effort has been the marvel of all succeeding ages, but none the less, it was presently followed by the tragedy of utter decay.

The commanding philosophy of the age—that of the Stoic—was essentially determinist and circumscribed by pure Reason. Augustus sought to pass beyond it, and in his reforms the rehabilitation of religious belief occupied the first place. "Throughout his reign he was always ready to head a subscription list for the repair of an ancient fane. 'Templorum positor, templorum sancte repostor.' Thus Ovid addresses him in the *Fasti* as the founder of new shrines, and the restorer of the old, not in Rome alone, but throughout Italy and the provinces. . . . In 12 B.C. . . . he himself assumed the Pontificate, and became the active head both of Church and State. In all matters connected with religion there was no one more conservative or more national than he. While tolerating the alien cults and new-fangled superstitions that had invaded Rome, he reserved his most liberal patronage for what was venerable and of native growth. . . . He increased the number of the Sacred Colleges, added to their dignities, swelled their endowments, and bestowed marks of special favour upon the Vestal Virgins.

RELIGION IN ROME

Ancient priestly foundations and ceremonies which had fallen upon evil days, such as the Augury of the Public Welfare, the Priesthood of Jupiter, the Festival of the Lupercalia, and the Secular and Compitalician Games, he refounded and reorganised. He restored the worship of the Lares, the minor deities of the street and the home, by raising three hundred little shrines at the crossways and street corners of the city, and by ordering that twice a year, in spring and in summer, their modest altars should be adorned with flowers. Due honour to the gods, both great and small, such was the cardinal principle of Augustus in dealing with religion.

"And he had his reward, for the religion of Rome struck new roots deep into the life of the Roman people. It is one of the strangest facts in history that just at the period when there was born in Palestine the Founder of Christianity, which was destined to destroy paganism, there should have taken place so marked a revival of the old religion. Its genuineness is beyond argument. We have only to take note of the number of ruined temples, of the decay of the sacerdotal colleges, of the contemptuous and sceptical attitude of Cicero towards the State religion, to see how low it had fallen in the last days of the Republic. . . . But in the early days of the empire a profound change takes place. The gods enjoy a new lease of life. Men not only worship, they almost believe."[1] "In the Julian Forum stood the stately temple to Venus Genetrix . . . completed by Augustus after Cæsar's

[1] Firth, op. cit., pp. 206 et seq.

death. In the new Forum there arose the magnificent temple to Mars the Avenger, vowed by Augustus himself during the battle of Philippi, and regarded by him with peculiar veneration. . . . He erected the temple to Thundering Jupiter on the Capitol . . . and the great temple of Apollo on the Palatine."[1] "Augustus encouraged others to follow his example. . . . Marcus Philippus his kinsman raised a temple to Hercules, Lucius Cornuficius to Diana, and Munatius Plancus to Saturn. . . . Agrippa raised the glorious Pantheon; and near at hand was the temple of Poseidon, founded to commemorate his many naval victories."[2] "Augustus eventually recognised that the identification of himself with Rome and the empire for purposes of public worship, the close union, that is to say, of Church and State, was a source of incalculable strength to the Principate. He would have failed in statesmanship, therefore, had he not encouraged this idea and given it definite shape."[3]

We cannot suppose that this last consideration was lost upon the astute and inscrutable Augustus, and we know that it sank deeply into the minds of his successors. The question therefore arises: "Are we here in the presence of religious systems that essentially subserved the State, or of systems that were essentially cosmocentric?" The answer to this question is vital to our argument, for, as we have pointed out (page 75), in speaking of the justification of self-sacrifice in a rational being, "a

[1] Firth, *op. cit.*, p. 202.   [2] *Ibid.*, pp. 202 *et seq.*
[3] *Ibid.*, p. 213.

RELIGION IN ROME

rule of conduct that takes temporal things as an end will not suffice; a religion *ad hoc* will not serve." If these religions are cosmocentric in purpose, and yet the civilisation that rested upon them fails for lack of racial self-sacrifice, then our arguments are disproved. And if, on the other hand, these religions are geocentric in purpose, then it will be seen that racial failure is what we have to expect. The evidence, however, that they are geocentric, and what we have called *ad hoc*, is conclusive. Dr. W. R. Inge's fascinating work [1] deals chiefly with the first century A.D., and his opening sentence tells us that "the national religion of the Roman people was a part of the polity of the Republic," and (page 7) that "Piety towards the gods and obedience to the magistrates were duties of the same kind." Gibbon is not less outspoken. "The office of Supreme Pontiff was constantly exercised by the emperors themselves. They knew and valued the advantages of religion as it is connected with civil government. . . . They managed the arts of divination as a convenient instrument of policy; and they respected, as the firmest bond of society, the useful persuasion that, either in this or a future life, the crime of perjury is most assuredly punished by the avenging gods."[2] Even Mithraism, unquestionably the noblest of the imperial religions, and the one possessed of the highest ethical value, was entangled in political meshes no less than any other.

[1] *Society in Rome under the Cæsars.* London, John Murray, 1888.
[2] *Decline and Fall*, chap. ii.

"Mithra," says Sir Samuel Dill,[1] "was ready to shelter the idols under his purer faith. The images of Jupiter and Venus, of Mars and Hecate, of the local deities of Dacia and Upper Germany, find a place in his chapels beside the antique symbols of the Persian faith."

It became especially the religion of the army. The highest of the State-recognised religions was to be found where there was the most need for self-sacrifice, and whither the legions spread, thither they carried the cult of Mithra.

Indeed the Roman civilisation carried the policy of encouraging religion as an instrument of State to extraordinary lengths. Any religion would serve, and was admitted, on the one condition that its gods were interested in the maintenance of the existing civilisation, and subserved the purposes of the Roman State. Any religion that inspired a sense of obedience to the State, and that regarded temporality as an end, was welcome. The number of such religions in the Roman civilisation was enormous. Isis and Serapis and Osiris, Cybele and Æsculapius, foregathered with the gods of Rome; and the Lybian, the Olympian, and the Capitoline Jupiter were treated with equal reverence. The religious situation may be most fitly summed up in Gibbon's famous apophthegm:[2] "The various modes of worship which prevailed in the Roman world were all considered by the people as equally true; by the philosopher as equally false; and by the magis-

---

[1] *Roman Society from Nero to Marcus Aurelius*, p. 625.
[2] *Decline and Fall*, chap. ii.

RELIGION IN ROME

trate as equally useful." With but two exceptions, all the religions of the world of Rome had this in common, that they were geocentric, and the outward sign of this character was that every one of them acknowledged the deified emperor as a god and received in return the blessing and encouragement of the State. The geocentric character of the recognised religions becomes even more obvious when we study the policy that was pursued towards the religions whose end was not to be found within the borders of the existing civilisation.

Two stood aside, and not for them was the lauded "toleration" of the Roman Empire. One was the Jew, treasuring the words of Isaiah in his heart, and looking for One who, born of his blood, should make pallid the glories of Rome, and establish a kingdom of this world that should bring the millennium with it. His faith bound him in scorn of the idolaters without the pale, and held him to the service of the God of his fathers. The other was the Christian, esteeming the empires of this world as nothing, finding the value of life in a new birth unto righteousness, and welcoming death as the entrance into the kingdom of his Redeemer—a faith that, binding him in love to his neighbour, yet held him in a service that knew no earthly tie.

To the monotheistic Jew the worship of the emperor was blasphemy. Refusing to join in it, he had no part in the Roman Empire, and the refusal was odious to the Roman world. "The polite Augustus," says Gibbon,[1] "condescended to

---

[1] *Decline and Fall*, chap. xv.

give orders that sacrifices should be offered for his prosperity in the Temple of Jerusalem; while the meanest of the posterity of Abraham who should have paid the same homage to the Jupiter of the Capitol, would have been an object of abhorrence to himself and to his brethren." Caligula, who ascended the throne of the world in the year A.D. 37, and reigned for four years, brought the matter to a head by attempting to place his own statue in the Temple of Jerusalem. The attempt gave rise, throughout all Jewry, to such bitter and unanimous hostility that, upon the death of Caligula, it was abandoned.

Thirty-four years later, during the reign of Vespasian, came the destruction of Jerusalem by Titus, an event, says Dr. Inge,[1] "that was perhaps the most murderous of Roman victories." To quote an old author, Echard:[2]

"Titus commanded both the Temple and City to be entirely raz'd, by a Plow being brought over it. ... To this fatal end came the famous city of *Jerusalem*. ... Never any Siege in the World was more memorable, the Captives amounting to 97,000, and those who perished in the Siege to 1,000,000, according to *Josephus*."

Even that was not the end of the Jewish hope, but their final dispersion was not long deferred. Their very existence was an offence to the geocentric spirit of Rome, and the last tragic stand against what was implied by the Roman *imperium* followed in A.D. 134. The last of their national

---

[1] *Op. cit.*, p. 51.
[2] *Roman History*, vol. ii. p. 204. 1713.[j]

RELIGION IN ROME

heroes appeared in the person of the gallant Barchochebas. He was girded with a sword by the aged Akiba, the last of the prophets, and the chief and leader of the extremest anti-Christian Jews at the end of the first century.

Hadrian entrusted the work of destruction to Julius Severus, governor of Britain. "And tho' he gained the victory at last," writes Echard, "he would not have chosen many Triumphs at the Purchase of so much Blood. . . . The War was concluded in two years time with . . . the Death of 580,000 Men in Battels and Skirmishes, besides infinite numbers consum'd by Famines and Diseases, and their whole Land laid waste, which almost prov'd the Extirpation of the *Jewish* Nation. *Adrian* after this strange desolation banish'd all Jews out of *Judaea*, and by publick Decree prohibited any of them to come in View of that Country, or so much as to look towards their Soil or City."

Barchochebas was slain, Akiba was put to a cruel death, and a shrine of Jupiter was erected among the ruins of the Temple.

The fate of the Christian was no better than that of the Jew. But it is strange to find how completely the view that religion was a geocentric affair had become ingrained in the conceptions of the age. Thus, while the Jews were accused of "tumult," the Christians were charged with "atheism." Even Gibbon writes:[1] "The most pious of men were exposed to the unjust but dangerous imputation of impiety. Malice and

[1] *Decline and Fall*, chap. xvi.

prejudice concurred in representing the Christians as a society of atheists." To the Christians, that is to say, this world was an instrument and not an end; their purpose was cosmocentric and their lives given to the service of the Most High. To them this world and its religions were incarnate in the deified emperor, and in him they saw no less than Anti-Christ. Thus the charge hurled against them was that of "atheism." The Jewish hope was, indeed, intolerable to the empire, but it is only when we find the purely cosmocentric charged with "atheism" that we become witnesses of the real and essential struggle—the true antithesis of principle. It was seen that the geocentric life and the cosmocentric life were mutually exclusive, and the vital nature of the tremendous issue was recognised on both sides.

It would be superfluous to recount the history of the persecutions. Not once nor twice, but again and again, the whole might of the Roman Empire was put forth in efforts to exterminate Christianity. The edicts went forth at intervals from the time of Nero to that of Diocletian, and throughout the world horror followed upon horror. To the Christians the magnitude of what was at stake dwarfed all other considerations, and the individual life became of no account. Death was a little thing compared with the surrender that was confessed by burning a pinch of incense before the statue of the emperor. Tiberianus, the governor of Palestine, wrote to Trajan, says Echard:

"That he was wearied out in executing the

RELIGION IN ROME 121

Laws against the *Galilaeans*, who crowded to Execution in such Multitudes, that he was at a loss how to proceed."

Their indifference to life seems to have caused the greatest astonishment. Gibbon,[1] quoting Tertullian ad Scapuli, c. 5, writes thus: "'Unhappy men!' exclaimed the proconsul Antoninus to the Christians of Asia, 'unhappy men! if you are thus weary of your lives, is it so difficult for you to find ropes and precipices?'"

The only reference to the Christians that is made by Marcus Aurelius is not less strange. We quote from Long's translation of his *Thoughts*, xi. 3:

"What a soul that is which is ready, if at any moment it must be separated from the body, and ready either to be extinguished or dispersed, or continue to exist; but so this readiness comes from a man's own judgment, not from mere obstinacy as with the Christians, but considerately and with dignity, and in a way to persuade another, without tragic show."

Impressive indeed is the mental posture of Marcus Aurelius. An able man—a man worthy of the wide survey provided by his imperial eminence—he perceives only geocentric reasons for action, and yet is oppressed by a perception of the need of unworldly motive. Thus, while sitting upon the throne of the world, the note of his meditations is that of despair. "All things are the same—familiar in experience, and ephemeral in time, and worthless in the matter."[2]

---
[1] *Decline and Fall*, chap. xvi.
[2] *Op. cit.*, ix. 14.

The lapse of years has given us an even wider survey than that of Marcus Aurelius. We see that the Western world was woven into one proud empire, and possessed a civilisation that knew no rival. We see also the triumph of Reason. The civilisation is purely geocentric, the empire is an end in itself, and the cosmocentric element in religion is regarded as treason, and treason as atheism.

Here, then, we have the opportunity of testing the worth of the views advanced in our earlier chapters. If those views are sound, what have we to expect? What else than the exaltation of Society, followed by the decay of the Race, and the dissolution of the civilisation that it had created.

CHAPTER III

SOCIETY UNDER THE ROMAN EMPIRE

THE conditions of life under the Emperors of Rome is a theme that has occupied the pens of some of the most able men that have arisen in modern times, and the judgment that they have formed is strangely confused. It is a mixture of admiration and disgust: and it may be counted as a merit to the present outlook upon life that the sentiment of the majority of these judges is essentially one of disgust.

The confusion, however, is to a very large extent removed when we distinguish between Society and the Race. The racial conditions excite our horror. The social conditions—that is, the unqualified and unanimous determination to make the most of this life—created a society of unparalleled magnificence. Nothing was wanting: civilisation was consolidated under one administration, and the earth was swept to supply slaves and to furnish marbles and wealth. The ruthless social splendour, and the unrestrained gratification of the senses that resulted, produces a sense of stupefaction in the modern mind. To us, many of the actors seem unbalanced. When, in the pages of Tacitus and Suetonius, we read the record of the emperors and of the sinister women who stand behind them, we are oppressed by the feeling that we have entered a pathological museum. Regarding them from the standpoint of to-day, we seem to be contemplating a pre-arranged series, and feel that, although the objects differ from one another, yet a certain sameness pervades the whole. The catalogue introduces us to a number of different morbid specimens illustrating, nearly always, the same disease. To the ordinary reader of the ancient historians it appears that a majority of the characters portrayed were, more or less, persons of unsound mind, and that they ought to have been placed under restraint. In modern times it has been seriously maintained that the curse of insanity ran in the Claudian blood. But what, then, of the emperors, not less unbridled, who were not of the Claudian line? Frequently the emperors were not kin to one another, and yet the sameness persists. On the other hand, where the putative relationship is most close, there is, sometimes, the greatest contrast in character, as when a Julia is born to Augustus, a Nero to Germanicus, or the refinement of Marcus Aurelius is succeeded by the beastiality of Commodus. To regard a majority of a long series of emperors, and a majority of those who surrounded them, as insane, is to reach a conclusion that, on the face of it, is improbable; and in their contemporaries we find no trace of the sense of having been in the presence of the pathological. There is not even any evidence that they were unpopular with the commonalty of their day. The question of the restoration of the Republic does not seem to have

SOCIETY IN ROME 125

been popularly mooted. Sir Samuel Dill[1] says: "Suet. Claud. x.; Calig. lx.; D. Cass. 60, i.—On the assassination of Caligula, the Senate debated the question of abolishing the memory of the Cæsars, and restoring the Republic; but the mob outside the Temple of the Capitoline Jupiter demanded 'one ruler' of the world." And,[2] speaking of such a monster as Nero, "It is very striking, that, in the records of his reign, the most damning accusation against him is that he disgraced the purple by exhibitions on the stage." At the worst, the emperors were not destroyed by any revolt of their subjects excited by general hostility, although they frequently suffered private assassination as the result of a palace intrigue. It is not until the time of Heliogabalus, some two hundred years after the birth of Christianity, that we find the self-indulgence of the emperors exciting really widespread disgust. Gradually we reach the conclusion that, abnormal as they and their associates appear to us, they were normal to the age in which they lived. We are contemplating a temper of mind almost inconceivable to ourselves; to exercise restraint was to waste the fleeting days; gratification of the senses was the aim of life.

If we leave the emperors and their satellites, and successively pass in review the lower grades of the social scale, we meet persistently with the same spirit. Everywhere we encounter the work

[1] *Roman Society from Nero to Marcus Aurelius* (Macmillan, 1904), in a footnote on page 38.
[2] *Op. cit.*, p. 19.

of pure Reason; we find that interest is dominant, and that *carpe diem* is the rule of life. Many of the most splendid and enduring monuments of Roman art and architecture are theatres, baths, and other municipal structures erected for the delectation of the populace, and the area that was subject to Rome is still covered by ruins that attest the spirit, not of work, but of play. The municipality supplants the family, and the local amphitheatre is the structure that survives. " Men looked for their happiness to their city rather than to the family or to the State . . . and the buildings and banquets and bright festivals on which so much was lavished, were enjoyed by all citizens alike, the lowest and the highest, although high and low had sometimes by prescriptive usage an unequal share in the largesses. The free enjoyment of sumptuous baths, of good water from the Atlas, the Apennines, or the Alban Hills; the right to sit at ease with one's fellows when the *Pseudolus* or the *Adelphi* was put on the boards; the pleasure of strolling in the shady colonnades of the forum or the market, surrounded by brilliant marbles and frescoes, with fountains shedding their coolness around; the good fellowship which, for the time, levelled all ranks, in many a simple communal feast, with a coin or two distributed at the end to recall or heighten the pleasure; all these things tended to make the city a true home, to some extent almost a great family circle. . . . The love of amusement grew upon the Roman character as civilisation developed in organisation and splendour, and unfortunately the favourite amusements were

SOCIETY IN ROME 127

often obscene and cruel. The calendar of the time is sufficiently ominous. The number of days which were annually given up to games and spectacles at Rome rose from 66 in the reign of Augustus to 135 in the reign of M. Aurelius, and to 175 or more in the fourth century. In this reckoning, no account is taken of extraordinary festivals on special occasions. . . . The lubricity of pantomime and the slaughter of the arena were never more fiercely and keenly enjoyed than when the Germans were thundering at the gates of Treves and Carthage."[1]

If we turn to the literature of the age we find the same record. We may, perhaps, think that it would be unjust to accept the descriptions of Juvenal, Martial, and Petronius as pictures of the ordinary conditions of life among the well-to-do, and, if so, let us judge the age by its ideals of goodness and not by its moral aberrations. Let us turn to the better aspect and to such moralists as Quintilian, Tacitus, and Pliny. What do we discover? We see that Quintilian (i. 2, 4, 8) finds it necessary to denounce the corruption of youth by the sight of their fathers toying with mistresses and minions. Tacitus (*De Or.*, 28) finds it necessary to preach the virtues of pure motherhood. The philosopher Musonius finds it necessary to teach that[2] "All indulgence outside the sober limits of wedlock was a gross animal degradation of human dignity." And we cannot suppose that the moral remarks of Cicero were

---
[1] Sir Samuel Dill, *op. cit.*, pp. 232 *et seq.*
[2] *Ibid.*, p. 143.

not brilliant to his contemporaries, although we find them the dullest of platitudes. Finding that the moralists themselves set up such very primitive ideals as these, what are we to think of the unrestrained pursuit of self-indulgence in the society that surrounded them? Just as we reached the conclusion that the monstrous emperors were not really insane, so we may infer that the amazing pictures drawn by Juvenal, Martial, and Petronius are not really preposterous. We shall cease to marvel at the indictment of St. Paul (Rom. i. 24 *et seq.*) or the denunciations of the Son of Thunder (Rev. xvii. and xviii.).

When we pass on to inquire into the conditions that prevailed in the relatively poorer classes, we find that the same tendency shows itself in measures taken with the object of eliminating competition. Socialism steadily grew within the empire, and had become a highly developed system when Diocletian divested himself of the purple in A.D. 305. The movement seems to have been widespread: in Acts xix. 23–41, for example, we find, at Ephesus, an organised craft with an accepted leader, Demetrius, and a " town clerk," who admits that there are certain causes in which the organised craft may take action. It appears to have begun with a blend of what, just at present, is called syndicalism, or trades unionism, with socialism.

Professor Flinders Petrie, D.C.L., LL.D., F.R.S., refers to these facts in a small book that he published with the title *Janus in Modern Life*[1]—

[1] London, A. Constable & Co., Limited, 1907.

SOCIETY IN ROME 129

a book that we have found one of the most interesting and most wholly admirable works that have been written in recent years. "About A.D. 230," he writes (page 30), "all trades were organised into corporations or trades unions, recognised by the Government, instead of being only private societies as before. This seems to have been a compulsory unionism; but there was some difference in class between this unionism and our own. In Rome the trades were in the hands of smaller men, and not of large firms and companies as much as with us; and, on the other hand, the mere mechanic was usually a slave, this slave labour being economically the equivalent of machinery in our time. Hence the Roman trades unions were small employers of the status of our plumbers or upholsterers, more than, as with us, a large mass of crude labour organised against all capital. They were trade unions, rather than unions of mechanics as against managers. The compulsory entry of all the master employers would no doubt be a step very welcome to modern unionism, and the compulsory extension of it so as to leave no free labour would be an ideal condition, while picketing would be quite superseded by legal compulsion to join the union. The differences, therefore, were such as our trades unions would desire and aim at in the future; in short, unionism by A.D. 230 was more developed than it is at present with us."

Thus competition between traders was eliminated. But this result was not all that was achieved. If on the one hand the State, by the abolition of free labour, granted a monopoly to the union, so, on the other hand, it exacted a consideration. Society, in return, required that a certain amount of work should be done either gratis or below cost. This work was to be done for the poor, all profits were to be earned from wealth: thus the competitive stress was relieved both to those within the union and to those without it.

"Early in the third century, the grain importers and the bakers, being two trades that touched the proletariat most closely, were organised as monopolist unions on condition that they should do a certain amount of work for the poor at a nominal rate. Each member of the union was assessed by his union" (we are quoting Professor Flinders Petrie again [1]) "on the basis of both his capital and his trade returns, and he had to do so much of the cheap work in proportion. Hence the wealth of each firm determined the amount of proletariat taxation. . . . Hence to each person the aim was to work with the smallest amount of capital, and to remove from the business all spare capital and invest it elsewhere. This naturally resulted in business being badly worked. The difficulty was met by the law that all capital once in the business could never be withdrawn; and all profits,—and later, all acquired wealth—should be kept in the business, so that the richer firms should do their full share of proletariat service. The results of these logical developments of unionism and help to the proletariat were that many withdrew altogether from unions, retiring upon a small competence rather than live under such a burden, and

[1] *Op. cit.*, pp. 32 *et seq.*

SOCIETY IN ROME 131

that there was a general decline of commerce and industry."

" Property having thus become the gauge of responsibility in the union, the only way to prevent desertions was to declare that the property was attached to the union permanently, and whosoever acquired it did so under the implied covenant of supplying the share of union work out of it. The result of this law was that no one with capital would join a trade union, as their whole property became attached to the union; and poor persons were not desired on unions, as they could not take up a share of the proletariat service. This condition was met by the law forcibly enrolling capitalists in the unions, and demanding their personal service as well as the use of their capital."

"By A.D. 270 Aurelian had made unionism compulsory for life, so as to prevent the able men from withdrawing to better themselves by free work individually. He also gave a wine dole, and bread in place of corn to save the wastrel the trouble of baking. In the fourth century every member, and all his sons, and all his property, belonged inalienably to the trades union. By A.D. 369 all property, however acquired, belonged to the union. Yet still men would leave all that they had to get out of the hateful bondage, and so the unpopular trades—such as the moneyers in A.D. 380 and the bakers in A.D. 408—were recruited by requiring that everyone who married the daughter of a unionist must join his father-in-law's business. And thus 'the empire was an immense gaol where all worked not according to taste but by force,' as

Waltzing remarks in his great work, *Corporations Professionnelles*, where the foregoing facts are stated."

The system seems to have been completed by what Professor Flinders Petrie[1] calls "the vast socialist decree of Diocletian, regulating all prices and wages throughout the empire. A maximum value was fixed for every kind of food—grain, wine, oil, meat, fish, vegetables, and fruit. . . . Meanwhile the wages of labourers, of artisans, and of professions were all equally regulated, so that the best men could never have their superior ability rewarded. The prices of skins and leather, of all clothing, and of jewellery were likewise defined."

We need not dwell upon the fact that, for the pauper class, not only were free doles of corn provided—a political device that is not to be dignified by the honourable name of charity—but also the means of passing idle days in the excitement of the horse-races in the Great Circus. In every class we have found the exaltation of Society, and, in the words of Dr. Inge,[2] " We may grant, probably we should grant, that the Roman understood the art of living better than we understand it; that he knew better than we how to make the most of all the pleasures under the sun, from the noblest art to the vilest indulgences."

History, showing us a population among whom the non-competitive system was maintained by any and every contrivance, reveals a leisured people, and corroborates the testimony of the

[1] *Op. cit.*, p. 37.   [2] *Op. cit.*, p. 275.

SOCIETY IN ROME

numberless ruins of baths and amphitheatres. Ease, it is true, was purchased by the loss of liberty, and it was found that the hand of the State was laid ever more and more heavily upon every man. But no mundane consideration—not the loss of liberty itself—could bring men back to a life of competition. The footsteps all lead one way; there is no sign of returning to the hard conditions of rivalry. But the reader of these pages will not be surprised by the fact that the great Roman machine provided a socialistic existence for the mass of the people. Ease was obtained for every class. Neither before nor since has pure Reason been so greatly in the ascendant, never has the kingdom of this world been so splendid.

CHAPTER IV

THE FAMILY AND THE RACE UNDER THE ROMAN EMPIRE

LEAVING our review of the character of Society under the Roman Empire, we find, before we can understand the consideration of the position of the Race, that the family, as the nexus between the two, calls for notice. We are apt to regard the family as we know it as a part of the natural order of things; and at first it is not easy to recognise that it may be based upon other principles than those that we know so well. In saying this we are only referring to the monogamous family: neither the polyandrous nor the polygamous household merits the name of "family"; and they have no bearing upon the matter before us. Two forms of the monogamous family are recognised to-day, one being the cognatic family, and the other the agnatic. The distinction is of great importance. The cognatic form of the family prevails among ourselves and is well understood. Seeing, however, that the agnatic form of the family has been in force during the earlier periods of Roman history and throughout the whole of Chinese history, disappearing in the one and persisting in the other, some description of it becomes necessary.

THE FAMILY IN ROME 135

Sir Henry Maine, in his work on *Ancient Law*,[1] says, " The old Roman Law established . . . a fundamental distinction between 'agnatic' and 'cognatic' relationship—that is, between the family considered as based upon common subjection to patriarchal authority, and the family considered (in conformity with modern ideas) as united through the mere fact of a common descent."

" Cognates, then,[2] are all those persons who can trace their blood to a single ancestor and ancestress ; or if we take the strict technical meaning of the word in Roman Law, they are all those who trace their blood to the legitimate marriage of a common pair. But who are the Agnates? In the first place, they are all the cognates who trace their connection exclusively through males; . . . all who remain after the descendants of women have been excluded are Agnates, and their connection together is Agnatic Relationship. . . . *Mulier est finis familiæ.* . . . None of the descendants of a female are included in the primitive notion of family relationship."

" If the system of archaic law at which we are looking be one which admits adoption, we must add to the Agnates thus obtained all persons, male or female, who have been brought into the family by the artificial extension of its boundaries. But the descendants of such persons will only be Agnates if they satisfy the conditions which have just been described. . . . We may suspect that it" (*i.e.* agnatic relationship) " would have per-

[1] Chap. iii. p. 59; 9th ed., John Murray, 1883.
[2] *Op. cit.*, chap. v. pp. 147 *et seq.*

petuated itself even more than it has in modern European jurisprudence if it had not been for the vast influence of the later Roman Law on modern thought."

Thus the essential distinction of agnatic relationship is to be found in the understanding that, on marriage, a woman passes exclusively into the family of her husband, and ceases to be counted as a member of the family from which she sprang. The resulting contrast between cognation, the form of the family among white men, and agnation, the form of the family among yellow men, is indeed a singular one. In the cognatic family it is a matter of extreme difficulty for a man to trace his origin for more than a very few generations; he has to take into account four grandparents, eight great-grandparents, and so on. Very soon he is lost in a fog of relationships, and a prolonged tradition of family descent is almost impossible. Practically he only recognises contemporaries who are immediately consanguineous with him. Thus the outlook of the cognatic family is horizontal; it is essentially a recognition of consanguinity among the living, and shows us the family in its contact with Society.

In the agnatic family, on the contrary, descent is absolutely direct, and becomes a matter of the utmost simplicity, for it is evident that it can only be traced from father to son, or from son to father, as in the genealogies given in the Gospels of St. Matthew and St. Luke. In the agnatic family the outlook is vertical; it is a recognition of the continuity of consanguinity between the generations

THE FAMILY IN ROME 137

of the past and those that are to come, and shows us the family in its contact with the Race.

The Roman world started with all the racial advantages of the agnatic system of relationship. The ancient and honourable forms of marriage known as confarreation and coemption are clearly of that character. The first of them, *confarreatio*, was the more solemn, and was the only marriage of a distinctly religious kind. The second, *coemptio*, was the highest form of purely civil marriage. In both of them, the wife left her own family, and passed under the power, the *manus*, of her husband; her property became his, and, being included among those who came under his *patria potestas*, her legal position was that of a daughter. There was also a third, a lower, form of civil marriage known as *usus*—a continuous cohabitation in the husband's house for one year, from which the intention to enter into a contract of marriage was inferred. This lower form of marriage was also of an agnatic character; the woman passed under the *patria potestas* of her husband.

For our present purpose the point that is interesting is the degradation in these forms of marriage that took place in the society that we were considering in the last chapter. The causes that, as we then saw, led to the revolt against the social stress, and that, as we shall presently see, led to revolt against the racial stress, rendered these contracts meaningless and intolerable. A steady process of relaxation took place, and, to render them acceptable at all, their conditions were made less and less exacting. Confarreation and coemption had almost died out by the close of the Republic, and under the Empire, in the most splendid period of Roman society, *usus* alone remained. Even that persisted in a debased form: the wife absented herself for three nights in the year from her husband's house, and the legal effect of this expedient was that she never passed into the power of her husband, her property never became his, her rights remained unimpaired, and this form of marriage, scarcely distinguishable from concubinage, was almost universally adopted. "Most marriages," says Dr. Inge (*op. cit.*), "were now mere civil contracts dissoluble at pleasure." "It has been pointed out," he continues (p. 181), "by more than one moralist that in times of national corruption the women are generally even more vicious than the men. It was so at Rome. . . . The mere fact that we find such expressions as 'cuius castitas pro exemplo habita est' speaks volumes for the corruption of Society. But on this subject we need not here dwell. It is only necessary to mention it in order to explain that strange phenomenon of Roman life, the unexampled frequency of divorce. Divorce was resolved upon on the slightest pretext."

But this was not all. Reason stopped at no halfway house. Society might make the bonds of the married state as fragile as possible, but that did not meet the demands of Reason. The aversion was from matrimony itself. "The large majority of men never married at all." [1]

After the freedom from matrimonial contract

[1] Dr. Inge, *op. cit.*, p. 182.

THE RACE IN ROME 139

that prevailed during the early period of the Empire, "the dignity of marriage," says Gibbon,[1] "was restored by the Christians." He is speaking of the times of Justinian: unhappily, the influence of earlier conditions was still too great to permit a reversion to the rigid line of agnation, and the cognatic form of the family must be regarded as a legacy of evil that the modern world has inherited from the later Roman jurisprudence.

Our thoughts pass naturally from the position of the family to that of the Race. Here also Reason was dominant. But the situation is rendered one of absorbing interest by the gigantic and unparalleled efforts that were made by Augustus to arrest and reverse the revolt against the racial stress. Every geocentric consideration was in his favour. The grandeur of the traditions of Rome appealed to the imagination of his people, and the splendour of Society called for their patriotism. He devoted himself to the realisation of his hopes to preserve the Race, and we find the explanation of his attempts to resuscitate religious fervour in his effort to achieve this end. The element of tragedy is imported into his work by the fact that it was foredoomed to failure. *Ad hoc* religion was inherently unable to compass a cosmocentric purpose.

The position that faced Augustus was an illustration of the manner in which a high civilisation and the ascendancy of Society can be attained by the sacrifice of the Race, purchased, as it were, by the expenditure of the racial capital. Dr. Inge,[2]

[1] *Op. cit.*, chap. xliv. [2] *Op. cit.*, p. 69.

referring to the prevalence of infanticide in the first century A.D., writes as follows:

"The destruction of a new-born infant was, according to some authorities, forbidden by law, but it was certainly common.[1] Parents, whose sense of pity prevented them from killing an infant, often exposed it, in which case it either died of neglect or was reared as a slave or a prostitute by persons who made a trade of the practice. The habit of 'limiting the number of children,' as Tacitus euphemistically calls it, was condemned on political grounds as tending to diminish population at a time when the human harvest was bad; but we do not find the moral condemnation which modern society passes on the practice, a judgment which is due to a new conception of the guilt of homicide, introduced by Christianity. The practice of infanticide was certainly highly mischievous at Rome in this period, and contributed not a little to the gradual extinction of the Roman race."

"Abortion," he says (*loc. cit.*), "was not discouraged by law, and was very extensively practised. The art was a regular part of the physician's practice, and was apparently well understood.[2] We find praises of women for not resorting to it."

Details of further aspects of such matters may be found in Soranus—one of an honourable family of physicians practising in Rome in the first century A.D.

---

[1] See Sen., *De Ira*, i. 15, 2: "Liberos quoque, si debiles, monstrosive editi sint, *mergimus*."

[2] See, however, Ovid: "Sæpe suos utero quæ necat ipsa perit."

THE RACE IN ROME 141

Dr. Inge[1] quotes Petronius, who says: "No one acknowledges children; for the man who has heirs is never invited to any festive gathering, but is left to associate with the dregs of society. On the other hand, the childless man is covered with honours, and passes for a model of all the virtues," and Dr. Inge adds: " So great were the advantages of childlessness that Seneca consoles a mother who had just lost her only son by reminding her of the greater consideration that she will now enjoy.[2] A man who married was regarded as hardly in his senses. . . ."

Early in his reign Augustus set himself to the task of reversing these conditions and rolling back the tide of time. His famous reform, the Lex Julia, appeared in 18 B.C. It was divided into three parts, whereof the *Lex de maritandis ordinibus* attempted to combat the increasing tendency to celibacy and sterility by a system of penalties and rewards. The penalties seem to have been chiefly operative under the laws of inheritance. Severe limitations were placed on the capacity of the unmarried to receive a legacy, and their severity was only halved to those who, although married, were childless. Property was to pass to those who had children. If a husband and wife had children, they could leave their possessions to one another; but, if they had no children, only a tenth part; and, if they had children by another marriage, they might leave to one another as many tenths as there were children. If a husband absented

[1] *Op. cit.*, p. 31.
[2] See also Tac., *Ann.*, iii. 25 : "prævalida orbitate."

himself from his wife, except on public business, he was deprived of the power to receive a legacy. Vacant legacies were inherited by the State. Two years were allowed to a widow or a widower before remarriage became compulsory.

The rewards were designed to render marriage and the possession of a family fashionable. Married men with families were selected for promotions, precedence in the theatre, and remission of taxation.

The second part was the *Lex de adulteriis*, and finally came the *Lex sumptuaria*. This last was designed to prevent the dissipation of a family fortune by extravagance; property was to pass to children.

In A.D. 9, Augustus promulgated the Law Pappia Poppæa, the greatest work of Roman legislation since the Twelve Tables. It was an extension and codification of the *Lex Julia*.

" Il donna," writes De Montesquieu,[1] "la loi qu'on nomma de son nom Julia et *Pappia Poppæa* du nom des consuls[2] d'une partie de cette année-là. La grandeur du mal paroissoit dans leur élection même; Dion[3] nous dit qu'ils n'étoient point mariés et qu'ils n'avoient point d'enfans.

" Cette loi *d'Auguste* fut proprement un code de loix et un corps systematique de tous les réglemens qu'on pouvoit faire sur ce sujet. On y refondit les loix Juliennes[4] et on leur donna plus de force:

---

[1] *De l'Esprit des Loix*, Liv. xxiii., chap. xxi.
[2] Marcus Pappius Mutilus and Q. Poppæus Sabinus.
[3] Dion., liv., lvi.
[4] Le titre 14 des fragmens d'Ulpien distingue fort bien la loi Julienne de la Pappienne.

elles ont tant de vues, elles influent sur tant de choses, qu'elles forment la plus belle partie des loix civiles des Romaines."

These laws were not permitted to become a dead letter. Julia herself, the only daughter of Augustus, the widow of Agrippa, the mother of Caius and Lucius Cæsar, and the wife of Tiberius, was convicted under the drastic provisions of the *Lex de adulteriis,* and banished, at the age of thirty-seven, to the barren little island of Pandataria. The sentence was never revoked, and she died in extreme want and misery. Her daughter, of the same name, offended against the same law, and was banished to a small island in the Adriatic. Neither was the operation of the law confined to such persons as the Julias. Tacitus[1] says that "Spies were appointed, who by the Law Pappia Poppæa were encouraged with rewards to watch such as neglected the privileges of marriage, in order that the State, the common parent, might obtain their vacant possessions." Some of these spies became extremely rich, and the system of "delation" assumed enormous proportions.

Nevertheless the law failed in its purpose. Tacitus writes,[2] "Not even by this means (Lex Pappia Poppæa) did marriages and the bringing up of children become more in vogue, the advantage of having no children to inherit outweighing the penalty of disobedience."

In A.D. 9, thirty-four years after the *Lex Julia* had come into force, Augustus received,

[1] *Ann.,* iii. 28.
[2] *Ibid.,* iii. 25.

says Echard,[1] great complaints "concerning the too great Number of the unmarry'd *Equites*, which in a great measure proceeded from the Looseness of their Lives. This, together with the fatal Example of it to others, appear'd a Matter of so dangerous a Consequence to this good Emperor, that he immediately summon'd the whole Body of the *Equestrian* Order; where, in the Assembly, he ordered the Marry'd and Unmarry'd Persons to be separately plac'd: Then observing the former to be much inferior to the latter in number, after high applauding of the Marry'd Sort, he told the other, *That their Lives and Actions has been so peculiar, that he knew not by what Name to call 'em; not by that of Men, for they perform'd nothing that was Manly; nor by that of Citizens, for the City might perish notwithstanding their Care: nor by that of* Romans, *for they design'd to extirpate the* Roman *name.* Then proceeding to shew his tender Care and hearty Affection for his People, he further told 'em, *That their Course of Life was of such pernicious consequence to the Glory and Grandeur of the* Roman *Nation, that he cou'd not chuse but tell 'em, That all other Crimes put together cou'd not equalize theirs: For they were guilty of Murder, in not suffering those to be born, which shou'd proceed from 'em; of Impiety, in causing the Names and Honours of their Ancestors to cease; and of Sacrilege, in destroying their kind, which proceed from the Immortal Gods, and Human Nature, the principal thing consecrated to 'em. Therefore, in*

---

[1] *Op. cit.*, vol. ii. pp. 44 and 45.

THE RACE IN ROME

that respect they dissolv'd the Government, in disobeying its Laws; betray'd their Country, by making it Barren and Waste; nay and demolish'd their City, in depriving it of Inhabitants. And he was sensible that all this proceeded not from any kind of Vertue or Abstinence, but from a Looseness and Wantonness which ought never to be encourag'd in any Civil Government. Having finish'd his Speech, he immediately increas'd the Rewards of such as had Children, and impos'd considerable Fines upon unmarry'd Persons, allowing them the Term of a Year, in which Space, if they comply'd, they were freed from the Penalty."

There is a strange commentary upon this speech. In the reign of Nero, fifty years after the death of Augustus, Tacitus attests that "nearly all the Equites and the greater number of the Senators betrayed a servile origin." This is much as though the financial department of our Civil Service were manned by the naturalised sons of aliens, and the greater number of the members of our House of Lords betrayed a similar origin. At a later period, even among the emperors, many cease to be of Roman blood.

For long the framework of the State was maintained by the constant influx of aliens, chiefly slaves from the East, and German invaders from the North. The manumission of slaves went on uninterruptedly, and was a State necessity. The slave had a right to certain private savings—his *peculium*—and with this could frequently purchase his freedom. On manumission, those of servile birth entered into the middle class of libertines

K

or freedmen, and, even in the time of the first Cæsars, it sufficed to be born free to be qualified as ingenuous, or native freeborn as opposed to foreign. This was decided by the condition of the mother. " And the candour of the laws was satisfied," says Gibbon,[1] "if *her* freedom could be ascertained, during a single moment, between the conception and the delivery."

Under these circumstances it is evident that the statistics which have come down to us are vitiated. If the Chinese were admitted into Australia, and their Australian-born children were reckoned as Australians, no deduction relating to the white race could be drawn from the figures of a census.

Still, we know that the relief to depopulation that was thus afforded was only temporary. Reason did not spare the newcomers, and multitudes poured into Italy, only to vanish, like a river flowing into sands.

History holds no record of a more courageous and magnificent attempt than that of Augustus to reconcile the interests of Society and the Race on a geocentric basis. His lifelong effort failed; the Roman world paraphrased the corrosive question that was asked by the Emperor Heliogabalus: "Can anything be better for a man than to be heir to himself?" and decided that nothing could be better for Society than to spend the inheritance of the Race upon itself. The legislation of Augustus could not traverse the strict logic of that conclusion. Twenty-six

[1] *Op. cit.*, chap. xliv.

THE RACE IN ROME 147

years after Diocletian stepped down from the throne, Constantine removed the seat of imperial power from the Tiber to the Bosphorus, and we find Lactantius, a Christian writer who was contemporary with both, bewailing the "ominous depopulation of Italy," and the crushing taxation that fell on the few survivors. Pure Reason had extirpated the great breed of the builders of Rome, and civilisation suffered an eclipse that lasted for a thousand years.

CHAPTER V

GREECE

THE history of ancient Greek civilisation is parallel to that of the Roman. We find the same geocentric quality in religion, the same character in Society, and the same disappearance of the Race. Essentially, the history of ancient Greece is the record of a brief period of intellectual eminence, and our interest is centred in the rapidity of the appearance of this high development of Reason, the astonishing perfection to which it was carried, the shortness of its duration, and the suddenness with which it vanished. The history of mental ability in Greece is that of a rocket. There is the rapid ascent of a thin stream of light, the brilliance for a moment, and then again darkness.

The period of intellectual productiveness in the Greek race only extends over less than 200 years, and yet it has set its mark upon the world ever since. The men who made the name of their country famous were born between 525 B.C. and 342 B.C.; before and after those years such distinguished names as those in the following list are few and far between :—

	Born B.C.		Born B.C.		Born B.C.
Æschylus	525	Thucydides	471	Demosthenes	395
Pindar	522	Socrates	469	Æschines	389
Sophocles	495	Hippocrates	460	Aristotle	384
Phidias	490	Aristophanes	444	Praxiteles (flor.)	364
Herodotus	484	Xenophon	444	Zeno	362
Euripides	480	Plato	428	Epicurus	342

GREECE

There is, furthermore, a consensus of opinion among modern scholars to the effect that, during this period, a general intellectual capacity was diffused among the worshippers of Athene that is not less astonishing than the number of the men of genius who were produced.

Two questions evidently arise. Firstly, we have to ask: " What was the cause that determined the suddenness of the disappearance of this intellectual splendour, and the shortness of its continuance? " Secondly, we may be permitted to ask: " What was the cause of its equally sudden eruption? "

In regard to the first question, we may point out that, although the writer did not intend it, there is a sense in which the 5th Book of the *Republic* of Plato, and parts of the *Politics* of Aristotle, may be read as an explanation of the disappearance of Greek civilisation. That disappearance is an occurrence which falls into its place along with other similar phenomena. We have seen it in Rome, and analysed its causation: we know that in Greece the conditions were so similar that a like result might be expected. There also the great breed died out. The production of its wonderful works ceases abruptly—in an hour the spring ran dry; and we find nothing in the record of Greek morals that debars us from the conclusion that the suddenness with which the extermination of the brilliant Race was effected stands in direct proportion to the pre-eminence in Reason that had been attained by its individual members.

Our second question: "What caused the sudden development of a Race possessed of such supreme intellectual ability?" is one that only concerns our argument indirectly, and yet is not so far removed from it that we can neglect it altogether.

Study of the literature and life of ancient Greece leads to a suspicion that efforts were made to breed the most successful Race. It may safely be said that the subject was certainly present in Greek thought—it was "in the air." It was much discussed, for their philosophers have left us the outlines of imaginary States wherein such an effort was to be carried out—wherein the abolition of social competition was to involve, naturally, the abolition of free sexual selection, and the substitution of a system whereby none but the most able members were to be chosen for parentage. Their offspring were to be supported and reared at the public expense, while the less able members, by various expedients, were to be prevented from contributing to the numbers of the State.

Dr. Bateson, in his great work on Mendelism,[1] makes the following remarks in his paragraph (pp. 303-6) on its sociological application: "The outcome of genetic research is to show that human society can, if it so please, control its composition more easily than was previously supposed possible. . . . The consequence of such action will be immediate and decisive." We cannot lay too much stress upon this weighty expression of opinion, and

[1] *Mendel's Principles of Heredity*, by W. Bateson, M.A., F.R.S. Cambridge University Press, 1909.

GREECE 151

the hypothesis that, in ancient Greece, eugenic measures were not only "in the air," but in operation, would explain the sudden eruption of a high development of Reason.

Nevertheless, as we have already pointed out (p. 54), the basis of a permanent civilisation does not lie hidden among the secrets of heredity, and no success in breeding for intellectual ability will, *per se*, suffice to reveal it.

Further examination of the records of ancient Greek life should be able to confirm or reject the hypothesis that the period of ability arose as the result of the selection of the more able for parentage, and the rejection of the less able. If it were confirmed, then we should see not only the immediate success of eugenic measures, but also their ultimate result in the prompt self-destruction of the Race. The whole subject is worthy of investigation by the modern students of "positive" Eugenics, for, to quote Thucydides, "History is philosophy teaching by examples."

CHAPTER VI

RELIGION IN CHINA

WHEN we turn to the enduring civilisation of the far East, we find that the conditions are the very opposite of those obtaining in the ephemeral civilisations of the West. The contrast is not merely one springing from superficial distinctions of manner and custom. It is so profound and so detailed as to have a startling effect upon the mind, and seems to have been arranged artificially and of set purpose. The impression produced upon a man of European origin, arrived in China, is not adequately expressed by saying that he is bewildered, or that he finds himself at a loss. The very foundations of life, as he has known it, have crumbled, and others have taken their place: the world's centre of gravity seems to have moved, and to be over his head. He has landed in another universe.

We must seek for the explanation of this phenomenon far down in the contrast between the religious atmosphere of the West and that of the East. The idea of Christian duty has been so far rationalised that there are many minds in which it is almost limited to our duty to Society. In China, on the other hand, the European finds himself amid a population whose sense of religious

RELIGION IN CHINA 153

duty, not less one-sided or less extraordinary than his own, is limited to the duty that is owing to the Race." The European and the Chinaman are, in fact, looking at opposite sides of the shield.

The mutual misunderstanding that follows is so complete that, to the European, the Chinese appear as a nation of materialists, and the most unreligious of peoples. The mistake is akin to that which led the Romans to accuse the early Christians of atheism: and the one charge is as baseless as the other.

The Buddhism of China is but a thin veneer that overlies Tao, the ancient core of Chinese belief, for the pantheism of Sakyamuni has been found compatible with the native worship. "Tao" means "The Path"—the path, that is, of the active and creative principle in the universe. The desire to live in conformity with this path is indicated in a subsidiary manner in the system of geomancy that is known as Fung-Shui, but is fully seen in the system of Ancestor Worship.

The meaning that this worship has for the mass of the people is not very easily realised by the white man, either from a study of the Chinese classics, or by conversation with Chinese *literati*. The knowledge thus acquired is apt to be purely external, and to lead to a presentation of the subject that is European rather than Chinese. The surest means of obtaining an adequate conception of the real belief of the Chinese millions is by an interpretation of the antique ritual that is actually practised in the temples. Many years ago, when in China, the writer had an opportunity of "worshipping his ancestors" in a much-frequented temple, and, as the experience occurred to himself, it is more convenient to describe it in the first person.

The chief priest and I, on meeting, vied with one another in courtesy; and my interpreter explained the desire that I felt to provide for my long-neglected ancestors. The most instructive part of the interview immediately followed. The priest politely inquired as to the number of my children. I could not then—as now—claim the title of Paterfamilias: I was not even married. These facts having been duly explained by the interpreter, the priest bowed in a conclusive manner that implied that the interview was at an end. Though young in years, I was not inexperienced in travel, and presently an *accommodement* was found, and I was dismissed to consult the temple oracle. My interpreter and I passed through several of the courts of the temple, and, arrived at the oracle, my candle was lighted and the ceremonies of the occasion duly observed. In the end I was furnished with a slip of yellow paper bearing Chinese characters. Fortunately for my purpose, these, as I afterwards learned, set forth that I was destined to be the father of "many children, sons and daughters." Armed with this certificate of fitness, I returned to the chief priest, and was permitted to proceed with the worship that was before denied to me.

Concerning this worship, it will suffice to say that it took the form of an expression of my reverence for those who are the authors of my being.

RELIGION IN CHINA

"If we can divine the true meaning that underlies this ritual and the conditions that control admission to it, we shall have arrived at an understanding of a faith that has built up an unshakeable civilisation, and through thousands of years has illuminated the lives of uncountable millions. What meaning, then, do we see in it? We see that it is filled full with the idea of creature and Creator—of the individual in his relation to the living and creative principle of the universe. The Chinaman, through the long chain of those, his own proximate creators, who have gone before him, worships the ultimate Creator. And, if the chain thus extends backwards, so also must it reach forwards. The chain of worship must not be broken; it must never come to an end. Only when he himself has assumed the character of a creator is the Chinaman qualified to worship; only by fatherhood, actual or divinely guaranteed, is he justified in appearing before his ancestors and his Creator, paying to them their due meed of homage. The chain of creation is one with the chain of worship, and to break the one is to break the other." The Chinese sense of religious reverence is expressed by the word *Hiao*, a term that does not admit of an English rendering, except by some such poverty-stricken translation as "filial piety." In the mind of a Chinaman, *Hiao* not only implies a sense of devotion to his creators and their Creator, but also the piety that provides the generations to come, lest the chain of worship should be broken. To break the chain selfishly is, to a

Chinaman, sin unthinkable. He knows nothing of the distinctions that we draw between the altar and the hearth: a sonless Chinaman has failed in the primary justification of his being, and is cut off from the infinitude and eternity that surround him. Fatherhood is his first duty and his only worth.

Such a religion as this is in no sense geocentric: the interest of its votaries is not considered—it serves no purpose of the individual, for (as we shall see in the next chapter) it breaks him as though upon a wheel. The interest of Society is ignored, it inculcates no obedience to the Government, and is no polity of the State, for the State can barely exist in its presence. *Hiao* has no social influence; social conduct is left in such darkness that there the Chinese have had to fall back upon the guidance of Confucius, who, outside his Tao-ism, obtained his importance merely as an ethical philosopher. It serves, indeed, the race, and its power is concentrated upon one point—the preservation of the family—upon overcoming, that is, the precise form of rational conduct that has destroyed the Western civilisations. This result, however, is no more than an accident, for Tao rules in virtue of its own authority. To him who follows Tao, the Path of Creation, racial affairs are lifted into the clear region of duty—he is brought into contact with the infinite; he serves in self-sacrifice, and his life acquires cosmocentric significance. Tao is not *ad hoc*.

In the Chinese civilisation, then, the governing factors are exactly opposite to those that prevailed

RELIGION IN CHINA 157

in the Roman, and we may look for results that are not less divergent. We may expect to see the impoverishment of Society, the invulnerability of the Race, and the age-long preservation of its civilisation.

CHAPTER VII

SOCIETY IN CHINA

When we come to examine the facts of social life in China, our *à priori* expectations prove to be true, and we find that, just as Society in Rome went to one extreme, so Society in China flies to the opposite, and that the splendour of the one is not less astonishing than the sordid squalor of the other. The narrow Chinese conception of religious duty is obeyed with all the intensity of narrowness. The land teems with humanity, but there is no suggestion of communism, and the social stress assumes a horrible severity.

The absence of any form of communism is most clearly to be seen in the contrast between the ancient or modern trades union and its Chinese analogue. The vast Chinese industrial associations consist chiefly, but not entirely, of unskilled labourers, and are not confined to men of any one trade. A bargain is struck between the workman and the agent of the association. Perhaps, in a remote village, a young workman agrees that his labour shall be farmed out by the association for so many years—generally six. He undertakes to go wherever the association sends him, and to undertake work of any description, and at any time. The association, on its part,

SOCIETY IN CHINA 159

contracts to lodge, to clothe, to feed him, and to maintain him in illness, or during unemployment, throughout six years. All this time he receives neither wage or reward, but the association engages, on the expiry of that period, to take him back to his native village, and then and there to pay him a stipulated amount in a lump sum. Obviously the expenses of the association are considerable; obviously also the man, far from home and dependent on the association, cannot take the risk of incurring the suspicion of slackness, weakness, or any kind of inefficiency that might enable the association to repudiate its part of the bargain. The result is that he is spent and spends himself without mercy. It would not pay the association to engage him for a longer term; too often his health and strength are broken at the end of six years. But the scene changes when he is once more with his family and receives his little fortune. Thereafter he joins the ranks of the capitalists: he can engage in trade; perhaps he buys a sampan—certainly he buys his wife; he becomes the father of a family, and woe betide his competitors!

Thus, in joining one of these combinations, the workman's very object is to equip himself for an after-life of competition—not, as in any Western system, ancient or modern, to protect himself against it. The contrast with the ancient Roman system detailed by Professor Flinders Petrie is indeed remarkable. Here is no State interference, no compulsion to join, and no monopoly of a trade. Not less remarkable is a comparison with the modern Western system. There is no effort to withhold labour; the association acts as a gigantic labour-exchange; men can be sent anywhere in any required number, and the skilled man is kept to his speciality. The employer contracts with the association, not with the man or men, to pay an agreed price for a certain work, and his dealings with the men are indirect. Neither strike nor lock-out can occur.

The severity of the social stress that obtains in China is terrible. It is almost impossible to read all the many works that have been published on Chinese life, but we have met with none more vivid or more to the point, nor one, so far as our own knowledge goes, more accurate, than an article in the *Century Monthly Illustrated Magazine* of July 1911, written by Mr. Edward Alsworth Ross, Professor of Sociology in the University of Wisconsin, under the title of " The Struggle for Existence in China." Any one who is interested in the actual life of the Chinese should read the whole of his paper. From it we take the following extracts:

" Most of the stock explanations of national poverty throw no light on the condition of the Chinese. They are not impoverished by the niggardliness of the soil, for China is one of the most bountiful seats occupied by man. Their state is not the just recompense of sloth, for no people is better broken to heavy, unremitting toil. The trouble is not lack of intelligence in their work, for they are skilful farmers and clever in the arts and crafts. Nor have they been dragged down into their pit of wolfish competition by waste-

SOCIETY IN CHINA 161

ful vices. Opium-smoking and gambling do, indeed, ruin many a home, but it is certain that, even for untainted families and communities, the plane of living is far lower than in Western countries. They are not the victims of the rapacity of their rulers, for if their Government does little for them, it exacts little. In good times its fiscal claims are far from crushing. The basic conditions of prosperity, liberty of person and security of property, are well established. There is, to be sure, no security for industrial investments; but property in land and goods is reasonably well protected. Nor is the lot of the masses due to exploitation. In the cities there is a sprinkling of rich, but out in the provinces one may travel for weeks and see no sign of a wealthy class—no mansion or fine country-place, no costume or equipage befitting the rich. There are great stretches of fertile agricultural country where the struggle for subsistence is stern, and yet the cultivator owns his land and implements and pays tribute to no man."

"For a grinding mass-poverty that cannot be matched in the Occident there remains but one general cause, namely, the crowding of population upon the means of subsistence" (p. 437).

"The traveller who, in dismay at the stories of the dirt and vermin of native inns, plans to camp in the cleanly open is incredulous when he is told that there is no room to pitch a tent. Yet such is the case in two-thirds of China. He will find no roadside, no commons, no waste land, no pasture, no groves or orchards, not even a dooryard or a cow-pen. Save the threshing-floor, every outdoor spot fit to spread a blanket on is growing something" (p. 430).

"In one sense it is true that China is cultivated 'like a garden,' for every lump is broken up, every weed is destroyed, and every plant is tended like a baby. So far, however, as the 'garden' calls up visions of pleasure and delight, it does not apply. In county after county you will not see altogether a rood of land reserved for recreation or pleasure . . ." (p. 430).

"No weed or stalk escapes the bamboo rake of the autumnal fuel-gatherer. The grass tufts on the rough slopes are dug up by the roots. The sickle reaps the grain close to the ground, for straw and chaff are needed to burn under the rice-kettle. The leaves of the trees are a crop to be carefully gathered. One never sees a rotting stump or a mossy log. Bundles of brush, carried miles on the human back, heat the brick-kiln and the potter's furnace. After the last trees have been taken, the far and forbidding heights are scaled by lads with axe and mattock to cut down or dig up the seedlings that, if left alone, would reclothe the devastated ridges" (p. 433).

"A Chinese city has no sewers, nor does it greatly need them. Long before sunrise, tank-boats from the farms have crept through the city by a network of canals, and by the time the foreigner has finished his morning coffee, a legion of scavengers have collected for the encouragement of the crops that which we cast into our sewers. After a rain, countrymen with buckets prowl about

SOCIETY IN CHINA

the streets scooping black mud out of hollows and gutters or dipping liquid filth from the wayside sinks. A highway traversed by two hundred carts a day is as free from filth as a garden path, for the neighbouring farmers patrol it with basket and rake.

"No natural resource is too trifling to be turned to account by the teeming population. The sea is raked and strained for edible plunder. Seaweed and kelp have a place in the larder. Great quantities of shell-fish no bigger than one's finger-nail are opened and made to yield a food that finds its way far inland. The fungus that springs up in the grass after a rain is eaten. Fried sweet-potato vines furnish the poor man's table. The roadside ditches are bailed out for the sake of fishes no longer than one's finger" (p. 433).

"The silkworms are eaten after the cocoon has been unwound from them. After their work is done, horses, donkeys, mules, and camels become butcher's meat. The cow or pig that has died a natural death is not disdained" (p. 433).

"In Canton dressed rats and cats are exposed for sale. Our boatmen cleaned and ate the head, feet, and entrails of the fowls used by our cook. Scenting a possible opening for a tannery, the governor of Hong-Kong once set on foot an inquiry as to what became of the skins of the innumerable pigs slaughtered in the colony. He learned that they were all made up as 'marine delicacy' and sold among the Chinese" (p. 433).

"Haunted by the fear of starving, men spend themselves recklessly for the sake of a wage. It is true that the Chinese are still in the handicrafts stage, and the artisans one sees busy on their own account in the little workshops along the street go their own pace" (p. 435).

"Still it is obvious that those in certain occupations are literally *killing* themselves by their exertions. The treadmill coolies who propel the stern-wheelers on the West River admittedly shorten their lives. Nearly all the lumber used in China is hand-sawed, and the sawyers are exhausted early. The planers of boards, the marble polishers, the brass-filers, the cotton-fluffers, the treaders who use the big rice-polishing pestles, are building their coffins. Physicians agree that carrying coolies rarely live beyond forty-five or fifty. The term of a chair-bearer is eight years, that of a rickshaw-runner four years; for the rest of his life he is an invalid" (p. 435).

"In Canton, city of a million without a wheel or beast of burden, even the careless eye marks in the porters that throng the streets the plain signs of overstrain. . . . The dog-trot, the whistling breath, the clenched teeth, the streaming face of those under a burden of from one to two hundredweight that *must* be borne, are as eloquent of ebbing life as a jetting artery. At rest the porter often leans or droops with a corpse-like sag that betrays utter depletion of vital energy" (p. 435).

"There are a number of miscellaneous facts that hint how close the masses live to the edge of subsistence. The brass cash, the most popular coin in China, is worth the twentieth part of a cent; but as this has been found too valuable to

SOCIETY IN CHINA

meet all the needs of the people, oblong bits of bamboo circulate in some provinces at the value of half a cash " (p. 435).

" Incredibly small are the portions prepared for sale by the huckster. Two cubic inches of curd, four walnuts, five peanuts, fifteen roasted beans, twenty melon seeds, make a portion. The melon-vender's stand is decked out with wedges of insipid melon the size of two fingers. The householder leaves the butcher's stall with a morsel of pork, the pluck of a fowl, and a strip of fish as big as a sardine, tied together with a blade of grass. . . . Careful observers say that four-fifths of the conversation among common Chinese relates to food. . . . Axe and bamboo are retained in punishment, and prison reform is halted by the consideration that unless the way of the transgressor is made flinty, there are people miserable enough to commit crime for the bare sake of prison fare " (p. 436).

" Here are people with standards, unquestionably civilised, peaceable, industrious, filial, polite, faithful to their contracts, heedful of the rights of others; yet their lives are dreary and squalid, for most of their margins have been swept into the hopper for the production of population. Two coarse blue cotton garments clothe them. In summer the children go naked, and the men strip to the waist. Thatched mud hut, no chimney, smoke-blackened walls, unglazed windows, rude unpainted stools, a grimy table, dirt floors, where the pig and the fowls dispute for scraps, and for bed a mud *kang* with a frazzled mat on it. No wood, grass, or flowers; no wood floors, carpets, curtains, wall-papers, table-cloths, or ornaments; no books, pictures, newspapers, or musical instruments; no sports or amusements, few festivals or social gatherings; but everywhere children, naked, sprawling, squirming, crawling, tumbling in the dust—the one possession of which the poorest family has an abundance, and to which other possessions and interests are fanatically sacrificed" (pp. 439–440).

Professor Ross's description reads like an account of a people who have reverted to the methods of instinctive life. The deliberate reduction of existence to the lowest level of possible endurance suggests to the Western mind that China must be filled by a population that is devoid of Reason. Nevertheless, no mistake could be greater than that. The men and women whose lives are spent under the conditions detailed above are possessed of high ability, and we venture to say that their average development, both physical and intellectual, is superior to that of the average white man. In stature they are at least equal to that of the European, and, to watch a group of almost naked coolies working in the tropics is to see the mask-like Chinese face set upon graceful, athletic forms that might belong to Apollo or Hercules. It is not easy to find statistics giving their cranial capacity as compared with others. But it has been stated, in an article in the *Pall Mall Gazette* of 19th January, 1883, that "the only statistics of Chinese brain-weight available show them to exceed all other nations

SOCIETY IN CHINA 167

in this respect. The average brain-weight of the males reached $50\frac{1}{2}$ ounces, and that of the females $45\frac{1}{2}$ ounces. This is an average not attained, so far as yet known, by any other nation, it being fully 6 ounces above that of the average negro, and $1\frac{1}{2}$ ounces above the European."

Intellectually they are even less easily estimated. Careless of the State, with no desire for the advance of scientific knowledge, averse from the co-operation involved in the management of large industrial undertakings, they are not to be judged by our standards: their ideals are not ours, and their thoughts are alien to us. But, when a fair contest of wits occurs between a Chinaman and a white man, it is generally the latter who suffers.

If the power of Reason is not wanting among them, it follows that the voluntary creation and stoical endurance of a toilworn system of life springs from supra-rational considerations, and that the sordid social life of the Chinese bears witness to nobility of individual character. It is true that the narrow creed leads to a straitened existence, but if willingness to incur supra-rational self-sacrifice be taken as the measure of the religious capacity of a people, then the Chinese must be classed as one profoundly moved by the sense of cosmocentric duty. We may see further evidence of this capacity among those Chinese who, with a wider conception of cosmocentric duty, perceive that all conduct is significant, and see that social duty and racial duty are complementary to one another, each, as was pointed out on pages

82 and 91, coming into operation at the point where the other would begin to be destructive if it stood alone. The faces of the Chinese Christians often wear an expression of saint-like spirituality, and their constancy under persecution at the hands of an exclusively racial civilisation has been worthy to take rank by the side of that displayed by the Christians of the Roman Empire under the persecutions of an exclusively social civilisation.

CHAPTER VIII

THE FAMILY AND THE RACE IN CHINA

IT would be difficult to exaggerate the importance of the fact that the formation of the Chinese family is strictly agnatic. The conception of a direct ancestry reaching from an immeasurable past, and followed by equally direct lines of descent extending to an incalculable future, is one that fires the imagination and gives an importance to the family that can only be realised faintly and with difficulty by any one who is merely acquainted with cognation. But even this is not all. Taoism itself takes nothing into account except the family; and, as we have seen, requires the long thin line of relationship that is provided by agnation.

Chinese civilisation, accordingly, is so organised that the agnatic family stands supreme, and every other institution is contributory to it. The Chinese mind, usually so incomprehensible to a white man, becomes perfectly clear so long as the latter remembers that the agnatic family is the beginning and end of Chinese thought and action.

Bearing this in mind, it is strange to observe that racial duty is carried out, and the Race maintained and magnified, only in spite of enormous current difficulties and disadvantages created by neglect of the complementary social duties.

Thus the want of any social element in the Chinese conception of *Hiao* leads to the enfeeblement of Society as a whole, as well as to the impoverishment of the individual life. The State and the feeling of patriotism count for very little. The difference in ideals between the West and the East is illustrated by the fact that the European who "dies for his country" has behaved in a manner that is unintelligible to a Chinaman, because his family is not directly benefited—is, indeed, damaged by the loss of one of its members. But when a Chinaman, in consideration of so much paid to his family, consents to be executed as a substitute for a condemned criminal, and is held in honour for doing it, then it is the white man's turn to be bewildered. The State, in fact, only exists for the sake of the family, and is not, as in the West, ancillary to Society. Its impotence, both at home and in the passing international politics of the day, is the natural consequence.

To the same cause we must attribute the Chinese paralysis in scientific research, and their failure in large industrial undertakings. These phenomena do not arise from lack of intellectual ability, but from want of will. In each form of enterprise the reward is doubtful, and, even at the best, is not confined to any one family. They make no appeal to the Chinese mind and ambition. Learning indeed is honoured, but the Chinese classics are devoted to the cult of *Hiao*.

The feebleness of the State is the first source of disaster. The Chinese official, for instance, uses his office to enrich his family, for his sense of duty

THE RACE IN CHINA 171

extends no further; and the State, even if it had the will, is too weak to prevent him from doing so. The result is that every kind of injustice and maladministration is rife. This, in its turn, leads to a popular spirit of turbulence that breaks out at intervals in rebellion and civil war. The racial destruction that results is stupendous. Professor Ross (*op. cit.*) says, that "Shansi lost five millions in the Mohammedan uprising of the seventies. . . . Kan-Su, Yunnan, and Kwang-Si have never fully recovered from the massacres following great rebellions. . . ." The civil war that we call the Taeping Rebellion led to an amount of destruction that defies any calculation that is even approximately exact. Beginning in 1850 and coming to an end in 1864, it lasted for fourteen years, and is estimated to have cost China 20,000,000 to 50,000,000 of population. Had such events occurred in Europe, the minimum estimate would be represented by the massacre of all the inhabitants of Spain and Portugal, and the maximum would be more than equivalent to the extermination of the entire population of the United Kingdom. We are better acquainted with the facts of the Taeping Rebellion than with those of any other, but again and again, Chinese history is marked by slaughter on a huge but unknown scale. Kiang-Se and Chekiang still show the marks of the Taeping massacres, but all these appalling losses make only a transient mark on the great flood of Chinese life.

Again, the weakness of the State is seen in the shocking mortality that follows in the train of famine. The people live so close to the edge of subsistence that there is practically no margin. The bad season immediately brings starvation upon the scenes—a contingency for which no provision is made. "In Shansi thirty odd years ago," says Professor Ross (*loc. cit.*), "seven-tenths of the population perished from famine, and . . . Shen-Si . . . lost three-tenths of its people by famine in 1900." But the effect of famine is as transient as that of massacre; presently the onward march is resumed.

The neglect of science and sanitation is another source of destruction. The infant mortality is well-nigh incredible. Professor Ross (*loc. cit.*) says that "Dr. M'Cartney of Chang-King, after twenty years of practice, estimates that from seventy-five to eighty-five per cent. of the children born there die before the end of the second year. The returns from Hong-Kong for 1900 show that the number of children dying under one year of age is eighty-seven per cent. of the number of births within the year. The first census of Formosa seems to show that nearly half of the children born to the Chinese there die within six months." Still, the whole of this mortality is not due to want of sanitation. To quote again from the same article: "Pasture or meadow there is none, for land is too precious to be used in growing food for animals. . . . The cows and water-buffaloes never taste grass, except when they are taken out on a tether by an old granny, and allowed to browse by the woodside and the ditches, or along the terraces of the rice-fields" (p. 430). "The use of milk is unknown

THE RACE IN CHINA

in China, and so the babe that cannot be suckled is doomed" (p. 439).

In addition to this, perhaps one female in ten is deliberately done away with at birth. This exposure of female infants must not, however, be confounded with the infanticide that prevailed in the Roman Empire. Like all other Chinese customs, it is governed by the interest of the family. Until she is old enough to be useful, a girl is a burden on the resources of the home; for, on her marriage, she passes entirely out of the family in which she was born. The payment that her husband makes on her wedding represents the cost of her upbringing, and so it depends on circumstances to determine whether or no it is to the family interest to preserve a female infant. Sometimes the same consideration operates in another manner. The writer was acquainted with a family belonging to the river-population. In their sampan was a merry little girl, no relation to the other children, but living as one of them. Ten or twelve years before, while sailing near the river-bank, the mother observed a deserted female infant. One of her little boys was then two or three years old, and she rapidly made up her mind that it would cost less to rescue and rear the infant as his future wife, than it would to buy him a wife eventually. The family interest had guided her.

The result is that virtually every girl of twenty is married, and that the "position of women" in China is assured. As may be readily imagined, the place of the mother in an agnatic family is one of much domestic dignity and honour. Thus, even the ghastly infant mortality cannot stay the Chinese racial progress.

Disease destroys the adult also; and, on the average, the adult life is about fifteen years shorter than among ourselves. China is the abiding-place of plague, and its plains are haunted by ague—ague, too, that is not of a benign type. In his own person the writer bears evidence of its virulent and persistent character.

Plague was destructive in the Roman Empire, and the damage remained. It has not been less destructive in China, but the damage is repaired. The same remark applies also to malarial fever. The appearance of ague has been suggested as the cause of the depopulation of both Greece and Rome, and the suggestion has received the endorsement of one so eminent as Sir Ronald Ross, F.R.S.[1] But if the Greek and Roman races did not recover from the ravages of malaria, it was only because other and deeper causes were at work. Ague is but one of the many destructive influences that the Chinese race defies with success.

So immense is the power of their unrestricted birthrate that war, plague, pestilence, and famine cannot prevail against it. The narrow Chinese conception of cosmocentric duty, although it involves Society in the horrible conditions that we

---

[1] See *Malaria: A neglected Factor in the History of Greece and Rome.* By W. H. S. Jones, M.A., with an introduction by Major Ronald Ross, F.R.S., and a concluding chapter by G. G. Ellett, M.B. London: Macmillan.

THE RACE IN CHINA 175

have described, nevertheless demonstrates our contention that obedience to supra-rational considerations is successful in the preservation of racial life and the permanance of civilisation. It has conferred perpetuity upon the Chinese race and civilisation—a civilisation that has persisted so long, and whose origin is so remote, that no chronicle runs to the contrary. It confers upon them to-day a population of from 300,000,000 to 400,000,000. If they are venerable on account of their antiquity, so also are they awe-inspiring on account of their magnitude and latent power to-day. They have, if they chose to do so, only to lift their hand to seize the hegemony of the world. But they do not choose to do so; imperial rule is not their object.

Assiduous only for the family, to them is superadded a permanent civilisation and the inviolability of the race. Thus we watch them moving, in myriads and millions, towards an end that they do not seek, and a destiny that none can see.

If we turn to other examples of long racial persistence, we find, invariably, that supra-rational motive occupies a dominant position in their history. We cannot do more than make a brief reference to two: the persistence of the Jew, and the long continuance of the ancient Egyptian civilisation. The Jew, unchanged from antiquity, has never surrendered the expectation that makes his race indestructible—the hope that the bringer of a divinely-ordered world will arise, sooner or later, among his children. The Jewish Law, quite outspoken on racial topics, is only the expression of the pathetic vision that lights up the life of the Jew.

The Egyptian, his old-world foe, only survives in the Coptic Christians of to-day. Yet we need not wonder that their civilisation remained unbroken for 4000 years and more, when we remember how large a space their religion occupied in their lives. And those who, marvelling and hushed, have traversed the pillared solemnity of Karnac and of Thebes, know well among the wall-sculptures, the oft-repeated representation of Min, the God of generation. The figure of the phallic Deity, impressive as it may be to a reflective mind, is unpresentable amid the proprieties of to-day; but, to the Egyptian he was one of the Greater Gods. Moreover, he stood alone among these great ones in that to sin against him was to draw down retribution. His emblem is the scourge. One-armed — single of purpose — he carries aloft the ever-ready thongs.

He is not less active among the nations of to-day; those that incur his chastisement still die beneath his blows. Of the company of the Greater Gods of Egypt there is one whose power has not waned. He is Min, the Scourge-bearer.

CHAPTER IX

THE INDISPENSABLE BASIS OF A STABLE CIVILISATION

"Jesus, upon whom be Peace, said : 'The world is a bridge : pass over it, but do not build upon it.'"

Inscription on bridge at Fatehpur Sikri.

ROME and China have furnished us with illustrations of opposite extremes: the one with an example of social splendour and racial failure, the other with an example of social degradation and racial persistence.

The conditions that obtained under the Roman Empire have shown that Reason is deadly to the Race, and that geocentric religion exercises no restraint over its destructive influence. The broad fact is, indeed, that in the whole range of history— in every age, and throughout all the world—there is no record of an enduring civilisation that rested on Instinct alone; on Reason alone; on any combination of the two; or upon any Religion that served their purposes. Passing, however, beyond these agencies, we have found in Chinese life an example showing the prepotence of the suprarational method over that of pure Reason. The example, it is true, is incomplete as an illustration of the whole method of Religious Motive, for Tao-ism, making no attempt to deal with the competitive stress, and recognising only racial duty, fails socially, and China is filled by a population that is brutalised by overcrowding, and rendered desperate by the struggle for food. None the less, it has shown us that an entirely racial Religion is able to perform its proper function by securing the preservation of the Race, and the permanence of its civilisation, and that a sense of cosmocentric duty is capable of restraining pure Reason. In the whole method of Religious Motive the interests of Society and of the Race would be reconciled by a transformation whereby the interest of each would disappear as an end to be gained—whereby the service of both would be converted into the means of performing cosmocentric duty, and all conduct would be held significant.

Yet we have to appeal to Reason itself to decide whether valid grounds for this transformation are forthcoming or not. For the supra-rational method no more destroys Reason than Reason destroys Instinct, or Instinct destroys Reflex Power. Here, however, we do not discuss whether a belief in the cosmocentric significance of conduct does or does not stand justified in the courts of Reason. We have nothing to do with the question whether this, that, or the other Religion is true, false, or non-proven. All such inquiries are outside the scope of our work, and belong to the domain of Theology.

Nevertheless it has become evident that a Religion that makes all conduct of cosmocentric significance is the one thing indispensable, and that mankind has to look, in the first place, not to

A STABLE CIVILISATION 179

the statesman or the politician, not even to the man of science, but to the theologian; neither to Law, nor to Medicine, but to Divinity. For if, upon the one hand, the cosmocentric significance of all conduct cannot be verified, then a civilisation that is both true and stable cannot be realised. Upon the other hand, if Reason gives us the assurance of the cosmocentric significance of all conduct, both social and racial, as a matter of fact, then Reason is not, indeed, destroyed, but is overcome by obedience: a lifelong self-sacrifice becomes compatible with it, and interest is transmuted into duty. Then, and then only, is it given to us to build up a civilisation that, marred neither by the racial death of Rome, nor the social death-in-life of China, will lead us to limitless achievement.

Yet, even then, a paradox remains.

In this, the method of Religious Motive, that which is temporal is never an end in itself, but becomes only the means of expressing the cosmocentric purpose of our lives. Thus a true and stable civilisation can never be more than a byproduct of Religion. It is to be attained by those alone of whom it is not sought; and we see that, in the long run, the world belongs to the unworldly; that in the end, empire is to those to whom empire is nothing; and we remember, with a sense of awe, the most astonishing of the Beatitudes: *Blessed are the meek, for they shall inherit the earth.*

INDEX

ACTION:
— all possibility of unselfish, is taken away by common ownership, 80
— based upon the faculty of drawing inferences, 24, 25
— Chinese thought and, 169
— cosmocentric, attains a permanent civilisation, 103
— course of, 4, 18, 29
— forcibly controlled is not significant, 86
— founded upon a disinterested basis, 48, 70
— geocentric, cannot attain a permanent civilisation, 103
— must be from within to be significant, 86
— of racial value cannot be based on reason, 70
— of reason in relation to competition, 36
— of society, 94, 95, 98
— prompted by religious motive, 94
— respiratory centre called into, 10
— self-interested, prompted by reason, 30
— springing from impulse, 30
— springing from the inferences of the individual, 30
— test of social value of, 99
— that is injurious to the social machine, 79
— that of the trustee, 101
— under the influence of pure reason, 94
— which has not the opportunity of being controlled by law, 86
— which may be self-instructive, 10

Action (Reflex):
— at the mercy of its surroundings, 10
— development of, 9
— disability of, 10
— example of method of, 9
— not merely useful but essential, 9
— the first of the successive methods of maintaining life, 9

Agrippa, 143
Akiba, 119
Allegiance:
— of rational individual is to himself and to his work, 84
— of supra-rational individual is not to himself, not primarily to his work, 84

182　THE FATE OF EMPIRES

America, 3, 53
Ancestor-worship in China:
— illustration of, 154
— the system of, 153
Antecedents:
— harmony of human social systems with their own, 44
— necessary to significance in conduct, 82
— of civilisation, 3
— the determinist is the creature of, 75
Aristotle, 149
Arnevatn, 44
Athene, 149
Athenian, 110
Athens, 5
Augustus Cæsar, 111-114, 124, 139, 142, 143, 145, 146
Aurelius (Marcus), 3, 110, 121, 122, 124
Australia, 146

BABYLON, 5
Barchochebas, 119
Bateson (Dr.), 150
Beatitudes, most astonishing of the, 179
Berlin, 60
Birthrate:
— an ever-falling, 100
— " corrected," of Berlin, 60
— decline in, 60
— failure of, 50, 53, 60
— France has the lowest, 53
— power of controlling, is a novel racial environment, 61
— power of unrestricted, 174
— reason in the matter of the, 62
— the German, 60
— the liberty to regulate the, 88, 91
— the racial evils and dangers attendant upon a low, 32, 56
Bosphorus, 147
Britain, 119
British Registrar-General:
— figures issued by, 53
Brown (Sir J. Crichton), 53
Buddhism of China, 153
Bureaucracy:
— a despotic, 40
— revival of despotism in the form of, 39

CÆSARS (the), 146
Caius Cæsar, 143
Caligula, 118
" Casarita " an example of inability to draw an inference, 19
Chain:
— of creation, 155
— of proximate creators, 155
— of worship (in China), 155
Chekiang, 171
Chemistry, 4
Child:
— no place for it under method of reason, 63
Children:
— Chinese priest's inquiries regarding, 154
— famine of, in France, 64
— living in sampan in China, 173
— nurture of, 31, 57
— of the Jews, 175
— Roman laws concerning property and, 141
— the future belongs to, 31
— the possession of legitimate, the qualification for the franchise, 99
China, 107, 152, 153, 158, 160, 166, 169, 173, 174, 177, 178, 179
Chinaman, 97
Cicero, 127
Civilisation:
— a high, 139
— a permanent, 67, 103, 112, 175
— a true and stable, 179
— advance of, 69
— age-long preservation of, 157
— ancient Egyptian, 175, 176
— ancient Greek, 148
— antecedents of, 3
— based upon interest, 73
— basis of permanent, 67, 74, 75, 151
— cannot live by reason alone, 66, 68
— Chinese, 110, 156, 169
— Chinese race and, 175
— consolidated under one administration in the Roman Empire, 123
— cosmocentric, 109, 115
— disappearance of Greek, 149
— discovery of underlying principle of, 4
— dominant influence in that of the white man, 100

184 THE FATE OF EMPIRES

Civilisation (*continued*):
— enduring, 177
— enduring in the East, 152
— ephemeral in direct ratio to its dependence on reason, 63
— exclusively racial in China, 168
— exclusively social in the Roman Empire, 168
— founded upon interest a flat impossibility if to be permanent, 64
— geocentric, 108, 109, 115
— indispensable basis for a stable, 177
— is everyone foredoomed to failure? 66
— maintenance of the existing, 116
— measure of the vitality of any given, 99
— not subject to a fixed law, 4
— of Europe and America in the present day, 3
— one that would be marred neither by the racial death of Rome, nor the social death-in-life of China, 179
— permanence of, 175, 178
— purely geocentric under Roman Empire, 122
— purely rational, foredoomed to decay, 28
— religion as the basis of, 73
— resting upon a utilitarian basis, 66; cannot endure, 177
— Roman, 109, 116, 122
— suffered an eclipse that lasted for a thousand years after the fall of Rome, 147
— supra-rational in character, 108
— that has already persisted for a long time, 109, 175
— that is our heritage, 4
— the existing, 3
— the highways of, 62
— the records of past and present, 107
— two great examples of, 107
— unshakable Chinese, 155

Civilisations:
— all Western, 66, 100, 156
— great ones of the West in the past, decay of, 5
— struck down one after another, 63
— the records of past and present, 107
— two great, 109

Claudian line of Emperors in ancient Rome, 124
Cleavage between the interests of society and the race, 56
Clement of Alexandria, 102
Coemptio, 137
Commodus, 124
Competition:
— abolition of, 36, 79

Competition (*continued*):
— abolition of, suggested in ancient Greece, 150
—   ,,   ,, under Roman Empire, 128, *et seq.*
— absence of, 39, 78
— all that the individual gains by, 85
— among a multitude of individuals, 40
— among animals, 20
— among contemporaries, 31, 51
— an internecine contest, 37
— and its reverse, 84
— and private ownership, 45
— between the individual and society, 45
— between traders eliminated under the Roman Empire, 129
— cannot be got rid of, except by getting rid of that for which it is carried on, 42
— duty of the individual with regard to, 86
— elimination of, 39, 42
— entire relief from the incubus of, 42
— example of, among swans in Iceland, 44
— for the absolute necessities of life, 16
— genuinely to the interest of the individual to abolish, 42
— how can it help? 82
— impulse to, 44, 45
— internecine and lifelong under the method of instinct, 17
— is it in the power of the individual to abolish? 38, 42
— is it to his interest to abolish? 38, 42, 49, 77
— life of, 101, 133
— object of eliminating, 128
— objectless under Socialism, 43
— problem of its abolition under reason, 36
— reward of success in, 43
— ruthless under instinct, 15
— still one of the two great factors in the stress of life, 37
— stimulus of, 39, 41
— stoical endurance of, 108
— strain caused by, 32, 56
— stress of, 16, 32, 34, 37, 46
— system of social, is instinctive, 49
— system of unlimited, 77, 81
— the self-seeking of, 79
Conduct:
— a new rule of, when in the presence of the infinite, 71
— a rule of, 75, 76
— antecedents that are necessary to significance in, 82
— avoidance of that which is injurious to contemporaries, 79
— change from geocentric to cosmocentric, 74

186 THE FATE OF EMPIRES

Conduct (*continued*):
— constrained is not righteous, however right, 86
— cosmocentric, 75, 76, 83, 178, 179
— cutting off the entail of life, 88
— disinterested, 63, 68
— each of the geocentric methods fails to confer significance upon, 82
— earthly, when it becomes an instrument and not an end, 76
— enlightened, of the determinist, 75
— futile to say that instinct still governs it, 53
— geocentric motive follows, 79
— individual, in a socialistic society, 80
— inferential, 30
— interest of rational, 68
— interested, 71
— invested with the dignity of cosmocentric significance, 76
— lawless, and constrained, neither significant, 86
— of determinist purely geocentric, 75
— of fatalist, 75
— possibility of unselfish, 79
— racial, 87, 89, 91, 93, 97, 101
— rational, 48, 49, 68, 156
— significance in, 81, 82, 86, 93, 101
— significant, 86, 97, 167, 178
— social, 81, 85, 101
— social in China, 156
— that is of ultimate interest to the individual, 30
— that is suitable to the environment of religious motive, 71
— that will be of racial value, 66
— unselfish, 76, 79
— with regard to the race, 90

Confarreatio, 137
Confucius, 156
Constantine, 147
Cranial capacity of Chinese compared with other races, 166
Criterion of statesmanship, 99

DARWIN, 18, 23
Death:
— a little thing from the point of view of the Christian, 120
— Christian welcoming, as the entrance to the world of his Redeemer, 117
— draws distinction between the individual and the race, 50, 52
— duties in England, 98

INDEX 187

Death (*continued*):
— individual in the presence of, 50
— -in-life of China, 179
— of a father is taken as an opportunity for plundering his children, 98
— racial, 13
— racial, of Rome, 179
— Salome asks how long it shall prevail, 102
Decay:
— all purely rational civilisations foredoomed to, 28
— cause of, 4
— forces making for, 6, 67, 108
— underlying forces making for, 45
Degeneration:
— of character essential to smooth working of non-competitive society, 41
Demetrius, 128
Despotism:
— a revival of, in the form of bureaucracy, 39
— presence of, in socialistic society, 41
Determinist:
— does not believe that conduct is pre-ordained, 75
Development:
— of reason, 10, 151
— of reflex action, 9
— physical and intellectual in China, 166
— sudden, of reason in Greece, 150
Diagram:
— illustrating growth and decay of civilisation, 7
— illustrating the interests of the individual, society, and the race, 35
— of parallelogram of forces, 7
Dill (Sir Samuel), 116, 125, 127
Diocletian, 120, 128, 147
Disability:
— arising from method of reason, 68
— of merely reflex power contrasted with instinct, 10
— peculiar to reason, 11, 67, 71
— second, one of reflex power, 10
— shared in common by reflex power and instinct, 10
Domesticated animals:
— a pair of martins, 15
Duties:
— English death, 98
— social, 169
— social, but no racial, under method of reason, 99

Duty:
— Chinese sense of, 170
— Christian, 152
— clear region of, in Taoism, 156
— cosmocentric, 76, 94, 167, 174, 178
— interest transmuted into, 179
— is it that of the individual to accept a competitive life? 77
— is it that of the individual to adopt a non-competitive life? 77
— is this in the power of the individual? 77, 87
— manner in which the individual can carry out his, 95
— of significant racial conduct, 97
— of the individual, 74, 77, 86, 87, 96
— owing to the race, 153
— racial, 92, 95, 96, 98, 167, 169, 178
— religious, 152, 153, 158
— social, 94, 152, 167
— society possessed of, 94
— takes the place of interest, 73
— the portion of the individual, 103
— to the family, 96

ECHARD, 118, 119, 120, 144
Education ("Higher"):
— of women in America leads to avoidance of motherhood, 53
Egypt, 176
Egyptians (Gospel according to), 102
Elimination of competition, 38, 39, 42
Ellett (G. G.), 174
Embassy:
— from Marcus Aurelius to China, 109, 110
Empire:
— after empire struck down by reason, 63
— an end in itself in Rome, 122
— is to those to whom empire is nothing, 179
— of Rome, 111, 117, 120, 123, 138, 168, 173, 174, 177
— Socialism under the Roman, 128
— society under the Roman, 134
— the family and the race under the Roman, 134
Empires:
— of Rome and China contemporary, 110
— of the past, 4
— of this world nothing to the Christian, 117
England, Socialism and a falling birthrate in, 61
Entail of life:
— continuance of, 51, 52, 53, 61, 88, 89

Entail of life (*continued*):
— interest of the individual to break, under method of reason, 52
— law of, 92
— must not be selfishly broken, 92, 102
— power to break, 53, 61, 92

Environment:
— change of, under Socialism, 43
— created by inborn impulse, 70
— created by instinct, 62, 70
— created by reason, 70, 71
— created by reflex power, 70
— new racial, created by power to control birthrate, 61-63
— of interest of society, 70
— of life widened by each successive method, 69
— of limitless wastefulness under instinct, 62
— quite different under each new method, 62
— relation of reason to its own, 70
— that does not admit of further extension, 70, 71
— that is not earthly, 71
— the new, of religious motive, 71

Environments:
— several, 70

Ephesus, 128

Eugenic measures:
— immediate success of, 151
— modern study of, 151
— probably adopted in ancient Greece, 150, 151

Europe, 3, 53, 100, 171

Experience:
— a word of no meaning to the plant, 18
— among Arctic foxes, 24
— cannot dictate to the purely instinctive animal, 18
— of no value without the power of drawing inferences, 20
— we have no, of the efforts whereby life is maintained in the animal world, 30

FAMILY:
— agnatic, 134, 136, 169, 173
— among many and various peoples is regarded with veneration, 97
— and the faith among the Chinese, 97
— and the race in China, 169
— and the race under the Roman Empire, 134
— as a link between society and the race, 96

Family (*continued*):
— as an institution attacked by death duties, 98
— belonging to the river population in China, 173
— Chinese assiduous only for the, 175
— Chinese girl passes entirely out of her own, on marriage, 173
— Chinese workman returns to his, after serving labour association, 159
— cognatic form of, 134, 136, 139
— descent of agnatic family absolutely direct, 136
— duty to the, is duty to the race, 96
— events connected with, are of racial import, 97
— fortune, and the *Lex Sumptuaria*, 142
— ignored in the polling-booth, 99
— importance to the Chinese, 169
— in contact with the race under agnation, 137
— in contact with society under cognation, 136
— interest, and the destruction of female infants in China, 173
— not directly benefited when the father gives up his life for his country, 170
— possesses an importance which extends beyond its threshold, 98
— preservation of, under Taoism, 156
— racial duty is focussed upon the, 98
— religious veneration of, leading to submission to racial stress, 109
— rewards to render fashionable, in Roman Empire, 142
— so much paid to that of Chinaman who takes the place of criminal condemned to death, 170
— society the protector of, 98
— State only exists for, 108, 109, 170
— supplanted by municipality in Roman Empire, 126
— Taoism takes nothing into account except, 169
— the agnatic, stands supreme in China, 169
— the coming generations of the, and the purely rational individual, 51
— the disappearance of the, and the race, 51
— the form of, among white men, 136
— the form of, among yellow men, 136
— the franchise an appurtenance of, 99
— the life of, is longer than that of the individual, shorter than that of the race, 96
— the nexus between the individual and the race, 98
— the nexus between society and the race, 99
— to strengthen the, is the aim of all right social action, 99
— two forms of, 134

Family (*continued*):
— under the Roman Empire, 134, 137-139
— wife leaves hers, and passes under that of her husband, 136, 137

Fatalist:
— believes that all conduct is preordained, 75

Fate:
— of present civilisation of Europe and America, 3

Fatehpur Sikri, inscription on bridge at, 177

Firth (J. B.), 111, 113, 114

Flaw:
— can we discover any underlying the methods which have failed to secure permanence? 17
— in instinct, destructiveness of, 20
— lies in the method of instinct, 18
— method of reason should have none that is inherent, 28
— that involves the wastefulness of the method of instinct, 19
— to make good the one in the previous method, 83
— underlying instinct, 17, 20

Force:
— authority of cosmocentric motive a decaying, 100
— making for decay, 5, 67, 108
— making for growth, 5, 67, 108

Forces:
— constructive and destructive in civilisation, 4, 5
— history gives resultant of, 5, 6, 101
— magnitude of, in civilisation, 5
— parallelogram of, 5, 7
— that have been in operation from the very beginning, 6
— themselves must be constants, 5
— those that we are seeking, 6
— two component, 6
— underlying, discovery of the, 45

France, 53, 61, 63

Franchise:
— an appurtenance of the family, 99

Fung-Shui, 153

Future:
— believed by fatalist to be foreordained, 75
— building up the, burden of, 52
— generations of the, 32, 33, 49, 56
— in which the individual has no part, 13, 51
— no mark left upon it by those who die before the age of parenthood is reached, 16
— not petrified by an external fiat, according to belief of determinist, 75

192 THE FATE OF EMPIRES

Future (*continued*):
— provision for, needless to society, 36
— provision that is of significance in the, 97
— the dim, and the individual, 95
— the living of the, linked to those of the present, 96

GAP:
— in instinct, 23
— left by instinct is filled by reason, 70
— left by reflex action is filled by instinct, 70
Generation:
— Min, the god of, (ancient Egypt), 176
— one after the other influences civilisation by the course of action that it takes, 4
— one after the other takes up the labour of instinctive reproduction, 15
Generations:
— future, provision of, in absence of competition, 32
— past and future, linked in agnatic family, 136
— provision of future, 49, 56
— the coming, 34, 51, 52, 88, 155
— unborn, and definition of terms "society" and "race," 33
— unoccupied areas await the coming, 31
Germanicus, 124
Germany, 60, 61
Gibbon, 115, 116, 117, 119, 121, 139, 146
Greece (ancient), 148–151, 174
Growth:
— force making for, 6, 67, 108
— of reason, 83
— promise of indefinite, under method of religious motive, 71
— relative rate of, of instinct and reason, 27
— underlying forces making for, 45

HADRIAN, 119
Hegemony of world could be seized by China, 175
— of world lately held by French, 64
Heliogabalus, 125, 146
Heredity:
— the secrets of, do not contain the basis of permanent civilisation, 151
Hiao:
— Chinese classics devoted to the cult of, 170
— cult leads to the enfeeblement of society, 170
— meaning of, 135
— no social influence, 156

Hiatus between interest of society and the race, 58, 71
Historians:
— Chinese, 109
— the ancient, and the Roman Emperors, 124
History:
— a resultant of forces, 5
— Chinese, 134, 171
— components of, 107
— different course might have been taken by, 65
— does not give the direction of its components, 107
— European, 100, 126
— failures recorded in, 35
— of ancient Greek civilisation, 148
— of persecutions, 120
— of the growth of reason, 83
— of the temporary renascence achieved by Augustus in the Roman Empire, 112
— recorded, 5, 6, 28, 29, 101
— reports only the end of the journey of organic advance, 6
— Roman, 134
— showing a non-competitive system, 132
— supra-rational motive occupies a dominant position in examples of long racial persistence, 175
— the shadows of, 28
— the splendour of man's achievements shines in, 28
Horace, 50
Horror:
— followed upon horror during the persecutions of the Christians in Rome, 120
— inspired by socialistic conditions of life, 38
— of socialistic conditions of life justified, 79
— racial conditions of Roman society excite, 123
Hostility:
— between the interests of the individual and the race, 52
— essential between reason and instinct, 83
— persists also between the race and society, 59
— reason not concerned to avert, 52
— Roman Emperors never excited any in their subjects by their conduct, 125
— to non-competitive life, 81

ICELAND, 44
Ideals of goodness set up by the moralists of the Roman Empire, 128
Illustration:
— historical, 107, *et seq.*

194 THE FATE OF EMPIRES

Illustration (*continued*):
— of coincidence of revolt against social and racial stresses, 60
— of conditions of growth and decay, 7
— of defence of the rights of property in the animal world, 44
— of difference between West and East, 170
— of individual ownership, 44
— of opposite extremes found in Rome and China, 177
— of principle of significance in conduct, 102
— of the flaw in the method of instinct, 18
— of the manner in which a high civilisation can be attained, 139
— of the movement in the direction of the power of drawing inferences, 23
— of the whole method of religious motive, 177
— of triangle of interests of the individual, society, and the race, 55
— use of parallelogram of forces as an, 5

Impulse:
— actions springing from, their relation to reason, 30
— gratification of, 13, 14, 29, 68
— inborn and unquestionable, of instinct, 14, 18
— of racial value acts by gratification of individual, 70
— purely instinctive animal dominated by, 14
— race acting by means of instinctive, 29
— that would spring into useful action in every emergency, 26
— to competition, 44, 45
— under control of reason, 27

Inborn impulses:
— environment created by, is that of the individual, 70
— foregone conclusions of, 29, 84
— gratification of, instinct knows no more than, 10, 15
— inherited, 12, 13, 17
— instinctive animal unable to do more than follow, 62
— method of, 70
— of instinct, 10, 12, 70
— possession of, 10, 70
— purely reflex world knows nothing of, 30
— self-sacrifice due to, 77

Individual:
— a servant under the method of religious motive, 84
  advantage of, decides between claims of society and the race, 35
— alone with the race in the region of instinct, 33
— as an instrument of the race, 29

INDEX 195

Individual (*continued*):
— attitude of the, towards the race, 95
— can only escape from the racial stress by avoidance of parenthood, 58
— can serve the race, 96
— Chinese religion serves no purpose of, 156
— competition between him and society, 45
— condemned by method of instinct, 17
— conflict between the, and society, 47
— death draws distinction between the, and the race, 52
— definite disadvantage to, under method of instinct, 15
— diagram of interests of society, the race, and, 35, 55
— divergence between his interests and those of the race, 56
— divided from society by competitive stress, 34
— does reason confer upon him the power to act in his sole interest? 53
— duty of the, with regard to the race, 87
— equal to society, 55
— greater than the race, 54, 55
— has but a brief span of life in comparison with the race, 50
— held in subjection to the race under method of instinct, 17
— hostility between his interests and those of the race, 52
— how does he fare under the method of instinct? 14
— identification of his interest with that of society, 55, 57
— if he lived as long as the race, 50
— if society takes the place of, 56
— impelled by instinct to the care of the young of the species, 14
— in contact with the race, 33, 34
— in relation to the creative principle of the universe, 155
— incurs stress of competition, 34
— instinct does not necessarily act to his advantage, 29
— instinct leaves no judgment to the, 14
— instinct secures his subordination to the race, 14, 25
— instinct subjects him to social competition, 49
— interaction of his interests with those of society and the race, 33, 34
— interest of, 30, 32–34, 42, 46, 48, 55, 95
— interest of, in relation to unborn generations, 34
— interest of society and, 34, 36, 37, 42, 50, 56, 94
— interest of the race and, 34, 54, 56, 59
— is it his duty to adopt a non-competitive life? 77
— is it his duty to carry the multiplication of the race to its utmost limits? 87
— is it his duty to perpetuate conditions of strife? 77
— is it to his interest to abolish competition? 38, 48, 49, 77

Individual (*continued*):
— is it to his interest to break the entail of life? 52
— is it to his interest to decline the provision of future generations? 49
— is it within his power so to frame his life that his conduct shall be of cosmocentric significance? 81, 87, 90
— is it within his power to avoid the racial a-morality of instinct and immorality of reason? 89, 90
— is it within his power to avoid the social immorality of instinct and a-morality of reason? 81
— lines indicated by interest of, 32
— lives in the presence of an ever-approaching death, 50
— logical position of, *vis-à-vis* to the race, 58
— marriage an act of madness on the part of a rational, 58, 96
— method of instinct costly to, 17
— minimum of reproduction on the part of, 57
— moral position in the absence of competition and in a world wherein all property would be vested in society, and nothing would be owned by him, 78
— moved only by interest, 51
— mutual dependence of himself, society, and the race, 94
— nature inflicts no penalty on, for childlessness, 51
— racial conduct of, 97
— racial duty of, its cosmocentric importance, 92; transmuted into duty to family, 96
— rational interests of, 35
— rational relations of society and the, 55
— rational relations of the race and the, 55
— reason at the service of the, 29, 34, 55
— sacrificed without mercy under method of instinct, 15, 17, 88
— secures for the race a future in which he has no part, 13
— self-sacrifice of, available under method of religious motive, 73
— separated from the race, but not from society, 34
— stresses that bear upon the, 32, 56
— strife between society and, 37
— subjection of, to society, 85
— subjection of, to the interest of the race, 48
— subjection of, to the race under religious motive, 92
— subordination to the race under method of instinct, 14, 15
— supreme power passes from the race to, under method of reason, 30
— the duty of, is clear under method of religious motive, 86, 96
— the purview of, future of race far removed from, 95

INDEX 197

Individual (*continued*):
— the term needs no definition, 32
— the transitory, 13
— to him it makes no difference whether the stress falls upon him as the father of a family, or as a citizen of a socialistic society, 58
— under the influence of religious motive, 92, 103
Individuals:
— acting in social concert, 94, 95
— existing sum of, constitutes "society," 33
Inference:
— "casarita" had not the faculty of drawing, 20
— man acts upon, drawn from observation, 31
Inferences:
— action springing from, appears under method of reason, 30
— advantage of power of drawing, 29
— faculty of drawing, 19, 25
— fox able to draw several, 24
— lack of the power of drawing, leads to wastefulness of life, 19–21, 62
— movement in the direction of acquiring the power of drawing, 22
— power of drawing, 10, 12, 20, 26, 28, 29
— purely instinctive animal knows nothing of, 30
— rational individual draws his own, 29
Inge (Dr.), 115, 118, 132, 138, 139, 141
Inscription on bridge at Fatehpur Sikri, 177
Instinct:
— a new faculty arises to remedy the defect of, 24
— a stereotyped inheritance, 29
— action springing from impulse stands to it as inferential conduct does to reason, 30
— advantage wholly to the race, 15
— advantages and limitations of, 12
— alone speaks in the imperative mood to an animal, 18
— and reason pull in opposite directions, 49
— appearance of method of, supplements reflex power, 70
— arose and survived, conditions under which, 62
— as a *modus vivendi* between the transitory and the permanent, 13, 17
— as contrasted with reflex power, 10
— avoidance of wastefulness of, by means of reason, 24
— "casarita" obedient to, 19, 20
— character of method of, 90, 92
— comparison of method with that of reason and of religious motive, 28, 29, 74

Instinct (*continued*) :
— condemns individuals to die in myriads, 17
— definition of, 12
— does not destroy reflex power, 178
— does not touch reason, 28
— element of liberty in method of, 85
— essentially a property of the race, 29
— ever-increasing power of reason as compared with, 27
— example of the limitation of, 19
— excluded by reason, 83
— flaw in, 17, 20, 24
— furnishes law against anarchy of method of reason, 91
— futile to say it still governs conduct, 53
— gap in, filled, 23
— gratification of impulse of, 13, 27, 68
great as are its advantages it does not provide any escape from the stress of competition, 18
— held in the leash of reason, 49
— history a complex of reason, religious motive, and, 29
— history of the overthrow of, 83
— hostility of the race to the individual is masked by, 52
— how far is the interest of the individual consulted under this method? 14
— how has it answered the problem? 13
— illustration of method of, 18–20
— impossibly cumbrous if asked to provide for every change of environment, 26
— impulses of, 63
— inability to deal with competitive stress, 72
— individuals impelled by it to the care of the young of the species, 14
— its racial a-morality precludes its adoption by religious motive, 89
— knows nothing but immediate impulse, 10, 13
— leaves no judgment to the individual, 14
— limitless wastefulness of this method is reduced by reason, 38
— method of, 12, 13, 26, 29, 67, 72, 76, 77, 87, 88
— no record of an enduring civilisation that rested on this alone, 177
— obeyed just as blindly as reflex action, 10
— outruns the limits of possible sustenance, 16, 30
— parental, 14
— parents the tools of, 15
— power of rational action superadded to, 25
— power to control birthrate absent under method of, 61
— purely an appurtenance of the race, 14

Instinct (*continued*):
— racial a-morality of, 88, 90, 92, 103
— reason does not destroy, 178
— reason does not exist apart from, 28
— reason the predominant partner in the association with, 27, 38, 46
— reason will overtake, 27
— reliance on, in respect of reproduction, 49
— social chaos of the method of, 82
— social immorality of, 81, 85, 88, 103
— strong though it is, it has fallen into the toils of reason, 53
— subjects the individual to competition, 49
— succeeds reflex action, 9, 62
— supersession of, by reason, 30
— tendency towards perfection of the method of, 26
— the constraint that ensures the continuance of the entail of life is absolute under this method, 52
— the enemy of society, 83
— the flaw lies in its wastefulness, 17
— the servant of the race, 83
— tyranny of, 15
— unable to dominate its environment, 62
— useful inborn impulses of, 70
— wanes while reason waxes, 49
— wastefulness of, 19–21, 37, 62, 63
— what are its advantages and disadvantages? 13, 14
— what is the common element of failure in methods of reflex action, reason, and? 68
— would come into its own again when reason becomes self-destructive, 83

Instincts:
— operation of two, 15

Interest:
— all unknown to purely instinctive animal, 12
— arguments put forward on the grounds of, 39, 40
— blank which separates that of the race from that of society, 71
— civilisation founded upon, is a flat impossibility, 64
— duty takes the place of, under method of religious motive, 73
— family, among Chinese, 173
— how does death affect? 50
— in carrying on the race, 56
— instinct acting in that of the race, 29
— interaction of that of the individual with that of society and the race, 33
— is dominant under reason, 126

Interest (*continued*):
— most complete expression of, is to be found in a socialistic form of society, 47, 63
— necessary disappearance of any civilisation based upon, 73
— of a socialistic society identical with that of the individual, 46, 57
— of all the living to break the entail of life, 62
— of every individual to eliminate competition from life, 42
— of society, 57, 70, 98, 156
— of society and the race, 58, 64
— of the individual, 14, 30, 32-34, 40, 45, 51, 52, 54, 79, 94, 95, 178
— of the individual and society, 42, 46, 47, 50, 55, 57
— of the individual and the race, 52, 68
— of the individual in regard to competition, 42, 48, 49, 77
— of the race, 14, 36, 56, 61
— of votaries not considered by Chinese religion, 156
— pure reason does not subordinate its owner to any consideration outside, 29, 30
— purely and inevitably a matter of, in a socialistic society, 78
— race acting in its own, by means of instinct, 29
— rational, 51
— reason acting in that of the individual, 30, 55, 94
— reconciliation of that of the individual with that of society, 60
— sacrifice of private, impossible in socialistic society, 79
— subordination of that of the individual to that of the race, 68
— temporal, is nothing under method of religious motive, 72
— the only guiding principle under reason, 71
— transmuted into duty, 179
— ultimate, of the individual, 30

Interests:
— geocentric, 95
— identity of, of individual and society, 58
— of the individual and the race, 52, 54-56, 59
— relative, of society and the race, 35, 50, 55, 64, 65, 178
— relative, of the individual and society, 34, 36, 56
— relative, of the individual and the race, 34, 48
— respective, of society and the race, 98, 146
— respective, of the race and the individual, 50
— those of society and the individual will not be at variance if both are confined within the same space of time, 36
— triangle of, 55
— whither do they lead with regard to stress of competition and stress of reproduction? 32

Italy, 112, 146, 147

INDEX 201

JEW (the), 110, 117, 119, 175, 176
Jews (the), 119
Jones (W. H. S.), 174
Julia. *See* Lex
Julius Cæsar, 111
Julius Severus, 119
Justinian, 139
Juvenal, 127, 128

KARNAC, 176
Keble, 3
Kiang-Se, 171

LABOUR exchanges in China, 160
Lactantius, 147
Lankester (Sir E. Ray), 15, 20, 22
Law:
— all social, excluded under method of instinct, 82
— and liberty, 86, 90, 92, 102
— element of, belongs to method of reason, 82
— enjoins that the entail should not be broken, 102
— failed in its purpose in ancient Rome, 143
— instinct furnishes racial, 91
— itself essential to significance, 92
— method of religious motive retains, 92
— none in unlimited competition, 77
— not permitted to become a dead letter in Roman Empire, 143
— obedience to the, only significant when liberty is also possessed, 92
— of entail of life, 92
— of inheritance under Augustus, 141
— of non-competitive method, 85
— of the one and liberty of the other method, 91
— reason furnishes social, 82
— retention of the element of, 85
— that justifies the existence of the individual, 92
— the Jewish, 175
— the opportunity of being controlled by, 86
— under which the individual has come into possession of life, 92
— unselfish liberty would take the place of, 102
Lawlessness:
— the very height of, 89
Lex:
— *de adulteriis*, 142, 143

202   THE FATE OF EMPIRES

Lex (continued):
— *de maritandis ordinibus*, 141
— *Julia*, 141–143
— *Pappia Poppœa*, 142, 143
Limpet:
— as an illustration of the method of reflex action, 9
Literature (Roman), 127
Long (George), 121
Lucius Cæsar, 143

MACHINE (great Roman) provided a socialistic existence, 133
Machinery:
— for significance in racial conduct, 93
— for significant social conduct, 86
— reciprocating, of a method of religious motive, 83
— that is perfect both socially and racially, 103
Maine (Sir Henry), 74, 135
Man:
— advance from protozoal organism to, 9
— at the head of the organic world, 28
   drawing an inference from his observation is able to make use of the processes of nature, 31
— pre-eminently the reasoning animal, 27
— to him the two stresses of life remain unaltered, 31
Marcus Aurelius. *See* Aurelius
Marriage:
— an act of madness in a purely rational individual, 52, 58, 96
— Chinese conditions of, 173
— " higher " education of women in America leads to avoidance of, 53
— in the Roman Empire, 137, 138, 141, 142
— that has not received religious sanction is regarded with doubt and contempt, 97
— under agnatic conditions, 136
— under religious motive, 96
Marry (to):
— the great racial act of a man's lifetime, 52
Martial, 127, 128
Matrimony:
— aversion from, under Roman Empire, 138
Method. *See* Instinct, Reason, and Religious Motive
Mill (J. S.), 64
Miocene period, 7
Mithraism, 115, 116
Mohammedans, 97
Montesquieu (de), 142

INDEX 203

Motive. *See* Religious
Musonius, 127

NATIONALISATION of property, 43
Nazarene, 97
Nero, 120, 124, 125, 145
Newsholme (Arthur, M.D.), 60

OVID, 112

PANDATARIA, 143
Parallelogram of forces, 5, 7
Parentage:
— selection for, in ancient Greek life, 151
Parenthood:
— avoidance of, alone can remove the stress of reproduction, 58
— self-sacrifice involved in, 54
Parents:
— are but tools under the method of instinct, 15
— exercise of the franchise should be the joint act of two, 99
— instinct subordinates them to the care of the young, 16
— must hunt for the insatiable young in the animal world, 15
— of the generations to come incur the stress of reproduction, 51
— only one pair of young can succeed to the position of, in the animal world, 16
— the life of, under method of instinct, 15
Paul (St.), 128
Petrie (Prof. Flinders), 128, 130, 132, 159
Petronius, 127, 128, 141
Pharaohs:
— Chinese contemporary with the, 110
Phenomena:
— similarity of, in ancient Greece and Rome, 149
— socialistic, 50, 60, 108
— twin, Socialism and a failure of the birthrate are, 61
Phenomenon:
— an intermittent, civilisation resting on utilitarian basis is, 66
— of Chinese paralysis in scientific research, 170
Physics, 4
Plato, 149
Pliny, 127
Portugal, 171

Power :
— assumption of, by the State, 108
— called into action by external stimulus, 9
— concentrated upon one point, in Taoism, 156
— conferred by reason, 27, 57
— disability of merely reflex, 10
— inherent in religious motive, 76, 84
— latent, of the Chinese, 175
— need of one that can act independently of a stimulus, 69
— of drawing a conclusion from premisses, 27
— of drawing inferences, 10, 12, 20, 22, 28, 70
— of husband in Rome, 137
— of inborn instinctive action, 24
— of involuntary response to an external stimulus, 9, 69
— of "looking before and after," 29
— of rational action, 24, 27
— of reason, 27, 37, 45, 48, 49, 62, 92, 167
— of reasoning, 20
— of religious motive, 76, 77, 84, 86, 87, 92
— of seeking the good of contemporaries, 79
— of self-sacrifice, 72
— of the individual, 32, 43, 49, 52, 77, 81, 83, 87
— of the methods to amalgamate, 83
— of unrestricted birthrate, 174
— of working for private advantage, 78–80
— reflex, 10, 62, 70, 178
— selective, of method of religious motive, 85
— superior to reason, 42
— that acts *ab extra*, 75
— to break the entail of life, 53, 61, 92
— to control the birthrate, 61, 91
— to deal adequately with the racial and social stress, 72
— to make good the disability of reason, 71
— to retain both liberty and law, 86
— wife passed under the, of her husband under *confarreatio* and *coemptio* in the Roman Empire, but not under *usus*, 137, 138

Problem :
— of the abolition of competition, 36
— of the maintenance of the race, 13
— the old, new problems raised by solution of, 69
— the standing, is to reconcile individual and race, 13

Problems :
— a series of new ones raised by each new method, 69
— the special ones dealt with by each method, 69

Progress:
— under method of instinct is wasteful, 17, *et seq.*
Property:
— nationalisation of, 43
Protozoal organism:
— advance from, to man, 9

QUINTILIAN, 127

RACE:
— advantage of instinct falls to the, 14, 15, 17
— advantage of reason is not limited to the, 29
— argument dealing with the, analogous to that dealing with society, 90
— attitude of the individual towards, 94
— blank that separates its interest from that of society, 71
— can only endure under a method which helps the transitory to act in behalf of the permanent, 25
— cleavage between the interests of society and the, 56
— conduct that serves the, 76, 90, 91
— continued under influence of instinct, 16, 49
— cosmocentric considerations require the individual to act unselfishly in favour of the, 95
— death draws distinction between the individual and the, 52
— definition of, 33
— diagram illustrating the interests of the individual, society, and the, 35, 55
— dim future of the, is far removed from purview of the individual, 95
— distinction between society and the, 33, 65, 123
— divergence between interests of the individual and the, 56
— diverse interests of the individual and, 55
— duty towards, 87, 94, 153
— earthly conduct concerning, has cosmocentric significance, 76, 89, 101
— has a future in which the individual has no part, 13
— hopes to preserve, Augustus's, 139
— hostility of society to the, 95
— hostility of the interests of the individual and the, 52
— if the individual lived as long as the, 50
— in contact with the individual, 33, 34
— in pure reason the individual is greater than the, 54, 55
— individual held in subjugation to the, by instinct, 17
— instinct a property of the, 29
— instinct an appurtenance of the, 14
— instinct the servant of the, 83
— instinctive individual held in subjugation to the, 15

Race (continued):
— instinctive method successful in subordinating the individual to the, 25
— instincts that concern themselves about the, 48
— interaction of interests of the individual with that of society and the, 33
— interest of the, in no way involved in reconciliation of individual and society, 36
— interest of society and the, 34, 35, 58, 64, 98, 146, 178
— interest of the individual and the, 34, 48, 56
— interest of the individual cannot be identified with that of the, 54
— interest of the individual separated from that of the, 14, 34
— inviolability of Chinese, 175
— invulnerability of Chinese, 157
— is injured under method of reason, 51
— is it the duty of the individual to carry the, to its utmost limits? 87
— lives in an ever-moving present, 50
— logical position of society vis-à-vis to, 58
— maintained and magnified in China in spite of enormous difficulties, 169
— maintenance of the, 96
— means whereby the individual can serve the, 96
— mutual relations of society and the, 94
— one that has disappeared, 110
— only the individual and the, 33
— organic advance and perfection of the, 17
— permanent, 13
— preservation of the, 88, 178
— problems of the maintenance of the, 13
— pure reason careless of the, 54
— pure reason the enemy of the, 83
— rational destruction of the interest of the, 61
— rational relations of the individual and the, 55
— reason deadly to the, 177
— reason would subordinate the interest of, to that of the individual, 55
— regarded as an organism possessed of indefinitely prolonged existence, 50
— relation of the interest of society with that of the, 35, 55
— relations between society and, 59
— religious motive retains law so far as interests of, are concerned, 92
— reproduction of the, 32, 34, 56
— result accruing to the, under reason, 48

INDEX 207

Race (*continued*):
— self-destruction of the, the result of eugenic measures, 151
— served by Taoism in China, 156
— society ancillary to, under religious motive, 95
— society and the, are guarded under method of religious motive, 102
— subjection of the individual to the, 48, 92
— subordination of the individual to the, 15
— sudden development and extermination of ancient Greek, 148–150
— supreme power passes from the, to the individual, 30
— the Chinese, 174, 175
— the demands of the, behests of cosmocentric religion higher than, 76
— the family and the, in China, 169
— the family and the, under the Roman Empire, 134
— the family in contact with, shown in agnatic relationship, 137
— the Greek, 148, 174
— the individual sacrificed to the, under method of instinct, 15
— the inheritance of the, spent upon society in Rome, 139, 146
— the most successful, efforts to breed in ancient Greece, 150
— the mutual dependence of society and, 56
— the position of the, under Roman Empire, 139
— the Roman malaria, 174
— the sacrifice of the, in favour of society in Rome, 139
— the unit of the, is not the family, 99
— the use of the word, will be only as defined, 33
— toll taken from the, by reason, 63
— uses the individual as an instrument under the method of instinct, 29
Race-suicide:
— direct incitement to, by death duties, 98
Reason:
— a tincture of, co-existing with instinct, 12, 22
— acting in the interest of the individual, 30
— action of society under the method of, 94
— advantage of this method is that it waits on the individual, 29
— a method entitled to take precedence of, 66
— a population devoid of, 166
— an animal endowed with power of rational action will make itself master of the world, 27
— and instinct pull in opposite directions, 49
— appeal is ultimately to, 178

Reason (*continued*):
— arose to remedy the flaw in instinct, and filled the gap left by it, 62, 70
— as a geocentric method, 84
— as a *modus vivendi* between the transitory and the permanent, 13
— at the service of the individual, 34
— blankly a-moral, 80
— can it state the terms of the mutual dependence of society and the race? 56
— can this method be justified? 35
— careless of the race, 54
— character of, 90, 92
— civilisation is ephemeral in direct ratio to its dependence on, 63
— compelling French society to advance to racial doom, 64
— competition from point of view of, 41, 42
— condemnation of method of, 60
— condemned if it does not afford a basis for a stable civilisation, 35
— confers power to break the entail of life, 53
— deadly to the race, 177
— definition of, 28
— desires identification of interest of individual with that of society, 55
— development of, rapid in ancient Greece, 148, 151
— did not spare new-comers in Roman Empire, 146
— disability special to, 67, 71
— does not exist apart from instinct, 28
— does not lend herself to equivocation, 57
— does not subordinate the individual to any considerations outside his own interest, 29, 30
— dominant in Roman Empire, 139
— environment created by, 70, 71
— ever-increasing power of, as compared with instinct, 27
— example of movement in the direction of drawing inferences, 22–24
— extirpated the great breed of Rome, 147
— failure of, to reconcile interests of individual and the race, 54, 56
— family not justified under, 98
— first achieved predominance by reducing the limitless waste in the method of instinct, 38
— frees the individual from both stresses, 49
— generally found in conjunction with some form of religious motive, 28

Reason (*continued*):
— gift of, is the true means of subduing surroundings, 31
— gives power to break the entail of life, 92
— gives power to control the birthrate, 61, 88
— gulf between primarily rational and primarily instinctive, 27
— has already wrought an immense change, 37
— has created, but left unsatisfied, the need of a basis of racial action, 70
— has made the human being the overlord of creation, and, in him, has attained the overlordship over instinct, 27
— has no racial quality, 52
— highest expression of, is to be found in socialism, 46, 61
— history a complex of instinct, religious motive, and, 29
— history of the growth of, 83
— hostility of society to the race under the method of, 95
— how can this method help? 31, 82
— how will it deal with the two permanent stresses? 31
— humanity circumscribed by, in absence of freedom of the will, 75
— if man is absolutely dependent upon it this method should have no flaw, 28
— imperious, demands total abolition of the two stresses of life, 57
— in relation to competition, 36, 48, 61
— in relation to reproduction, 48
— in the ascendant in Rome, 133
— in the matter of the birthrate, 62
— incompetent because it does not provide a place for disinterested conduct, 68
— inevitable work of, is to break the entail of life, 62
— inferential conduct stands in the same relation to it that impulsive action stands to instinct, 30
— inferential power of, 45
— instinct fallen into the toils of, 53
— instinct held in the leash of, 49
— interests of society and, 98
— is it competent to abolish competition? 38
— is not destroyed by religious motive, 179
— is the method that judges by interest, 39
— judged by the cosmocentric standard, 89
— limitations that make it incompetent, 72
— loses its old-time cogency, 79
— magnifies its office, 63
— marred by a disability peculiar to itself, 11

O

210 THE FATE OF EMPIRES

Reason (*continued*):
— may be a sufficient guide if the interests of the individual and the race can be reconciled, 36
— method of, 29, 35, 42, 66, 67, 72, 76, 84, 85, 89, 95, 101
— method of, fails racially, 66
— modicum of, possessed by modern animals, 20
— moral aspect of method, 88
— must advance on lines indicated by the interest of the individual, 32
— no record of an enduring civilisation that rested on, 177
— not discarded, but new method superimposed over, 68
— office of, is to prevent waste, 46
— only in rational world that conduct that is of ultimate interest to the individual appears, 30, 32
— philosophy of Stoic was circumscribed by, 112
— power of, 37, 48, 167
— pre-eminence in, among ancient Greeks, 149
— prepotent, would become self-destructive, 83
— progressively increasing ascendancy of, 45
— provides a short cut to advantageous position, 26
— provides racial liberty, 91
— racial anarchy of, 91
— racial destruction at the bidding of, 61
— racial immorality and social a-morality of, 89, 103
— racial immorality of, precludes its adoption by religious motive, 89
— racial insolvency of, 65
— racial liberty of, 92
— racially discredited method of, 78
— relation of, to its own environment, 70
— relations with social stress, 77
— removal of both stresses demanded by, 58
— retention of element of law under, 85
— reverses conditions of instinctive life, 30
— scope of, 29
— seems to lose its old-time cogency when advocating non-competitive conditions, 38
— sense of cosmocentric duty capable of restraining, 178
— social a-morality of, obviated by religious motive, 85
— socialism the highest expression of, 46, 61
— socially a-moral character and method of, 81
— still operative, 38
— stopped at no halfway house in ancient Rome, 138
— succeeds instinct, 12

INDEX 211

Reason (continued):
— supra-rational method no more destroys it than this method destroys instinct, but is superimposed over it, 68, 178
— taking all the earth for its province, 71
— the courts of, the method of religious motive in, 178
— the demands of, effect upon marriage in Rome, 138
— the enemy of the race, 83
— the interests of the individual and the race cannot be identified, because under this method the individual is greater than the race, 54
— the power to make good the special disability of, 71
— the e n partner in the association with instinct, 46pr domi ant
— the prepotent factor, 45
— the triumph of, in Rome, 122
— the very beginnings of, 20
— the work of, 125, 126
— this method and that of instinct have failed, 67
— to palter with, 57
— unsuccessful in any attempt to reconcile interests of individual and race, 55
— want of, instinct fails for, 19
— wanton bidding of, 89
— wastefulness of, 63
— waxes while instinct wanes, 49
— what has been its action in dealing with the strife between the individual and society? 36, 37
— what is the common element of failure? 68
— why should it not substitute a non-competitive system? 38
— why should it stop with its work half done? 38
— will no longer be a slave to instinct, 27
— will overtake instinct, 27
— would subordinate the interest of the race to that of the individual, 55

Reciprocating machinery. *See* Machinery

Religious Motive:
— able to retain element of value in each of the other systems, 85
— and duty, 77, 95
— and non-competitive life, 78
— and purely competitive life, 77
— as a *modus vivendi* between the transitory and the permanent, 13
— as the basis of a permanent civilisation, 74
— attitude of society under the method of, 95

O 2

Religious Motive (*continued*):
— comes with its own authority, 84
— continuance of entail vital to, 89
— does not seek geocentric interest, 101
— evidence of ability brought by, 87
— has it failed? 100
— history a complex of instinct, reason, and, 29
— individual takes his own course in this method, 86
— influence of, on society, 94
— is wholly distinct from its predecessors, 74
— justification of method, 100
— law and liberty co-ordinated under, 92, 102
— liberty demanded by this method, 101
— method falls neither into racial immorality nor social a-morality, but is perfect both socially and racially, 103
— method of, 9, 13, 74, 85, 100, 177–179
— mutual relations of society and the race under, 94
— not directly concerned with geocentric interests, 95
— office of society under, 96
— point of view of, 90
— possessed of a quality that distinguishes it from its predecessors, 74, 83
— power found under, 92
— power of this method to deal with social stress and with racial stress, 73, 86
— reason dissociated from, 28
— reason found in conjunction with, 28
— reciprocating machinery of, 83
— relation of, to racial stress, 87
— relation of, to social stress, 74, 77, 78
— retains law and liberty, 92
— selective power of this method, 92
— society under the influence of this method, 96, 98
— standpoint of, 77
— would be equally stultified by the exclusive adoption of the racial element in either of the geocentric methods, 89
— would be equally stultified by the exclusive adoption of the social element in either of the geocentric methods, 81

Reproduction:
— *See* Stress, subheading *racial or reproductive*

Revolt:
— against both the social and the racial stress, 60, 100
— against the one stress, 60
— against the other, 60
— against the racial stress in Rome, 137, 139
— against the social stress in Rome, 137

INDEX 213

Revolt (*continued*):
— against the two primary stresses, 108
— of reason shows itself simultaneously against the social stress and the racial stress, 60
— the emperors of Rome not destroyed by any, 125
Riddle:
— of the Sphinx, 13, 17
Rock:
— limpet clinging to, as an illustration of method of reflex action, 9
Romanes (Dr.), 23
Rome, 45, 107, 110, 112, 116–118, 123, 139, 149, 158, 174, 177
Ross (Prof. E. A.), 160, 166, 171, 172
Ross (Sir Ronald), 174

SAINT PAUL. *See* Paul
Salome, 102
Scandinavian lemming:
— as an illustration of the flaw in instinct, 10
School:
— the newer, of economists, 32, 56
— the older, of economists, 32, 56
Schools:
— of thought, 32
Self-sacrifice:
— a life-long, circumstances under which it becomes compatible with reason, 179
— a life of reasoned, 72
— an accident of, stable civilisation only possible as, 103
— in the service of Tao, 156
— of a rational being, 75, 76, 103, 114
— of inborn impulse, 77
— of the individual in favour of the race is not warranted by reason, 68
— power of, frees the method of religious motive from the incompetence of the method of reason, 72
— the need of, revealed by reason, 71
Service:
— a life of significant, is the work of the individual under the method of religious motive, 84
— and freedom within the method of religious motive, 93, 102
— Jew held to the, of the God of his fathers, 117
— life that is significant is expressed in, 72
— of both society and the race under method of religious motive, 178

Service (*continued*):
— reason at the, of the individual, 29, 34
— that is a method of religious motive, 72
— that knew no earthly tie, 117
— the expression of conscious relation to the infinite, 72
— the life of significant, 72
— truly significant, 82

Sex:
— antagonism, 52
— each is apt to regard the other as the cause of its own undoing, 52
— the childless of either, and the franchise, 99

Significance:
— antecedents necessary to, are law and liberty, 81, 82, 92
— conduct invested with the dignity of cosmocentric, 76
— considerations that are of infinite, 73
— cosmocentric, 75, 76, 81, 83, 87, 90, 91, 101, 156, 178, 179
— each geocentric method fails to confer, 82
— element of liberty necessary to, 85
— entailed, 89
— in conduct, 81, 82
— in each of the geocentric methods, 85, 92
— in racial conduct, 101
— in social conduct, 85, 101
— liberty and law essential to, 81, 82, 92
— life of, 77, 87
— lives of, that are to follow after us, 88
— of conduct under the method of religious motive, 86
— of life, 72, 85, 87, 89
— of life is life itself, 79
— of life of individual, 85
— provision of, 96, 97
— provision or non-provision of, 89
— racial, 91, 93
— standard of cosmocentric, 103
— the region of, Salome's question raised into, 102
— the very existence of, in the future is at stake in racial conduct, 89

Socialism:
— blend of, with syndicalism under Roman Empire, 128
— German, 60
— in the Roman Empire, 128, *et seq.*
— means the identification of the interests of the individual with those of society, 57
— ordinary definition of, 43
— prominence of, and a falling birthrate, 100

INDEX 215

Society:
— a communistic, 58, 63, 96
— a member of a socialistic, gains everything else, but has sold his soul, 79
— a non-competitive, 39, 40, 42, 58
— a socialistic, 49, 57, 58, 63, 79, 80
— acting in its own interests attacks the family, 98
— acting under the influence of religious motive, 95, 96
— and the race are guarded under the method of religious motive, 102
— argument dealing with, is analogous to that dealing with the race, 90
— as an organism, 36
— ascendancy of, under Roman Empire, 139
— blank that separates the interests of the race from that of, 58, 71
— character of, in the present day, 99
— character of, under the Roman Empire, 134
— claims of, 39, 76
— cleavage between the interests of the race and, 56
— competitive, does not require the individual character that is essential to a non-competitive, 41
— conception of, 33
— conduct that benefits, under method of religious motive, 76
— conflict between the individual and, 47
— consideration of relative interests of individual and, 33, 34
— co-ordination of work necessary to carry on, 40
— corporate action of, with regard to the family, 98
— definition of, 33
— degradation in forms of marriage in, under Roman Empire, 137
— diagrammatic illustration of triangle of interests of the individual, the race, and, 35, 55
— distinction between the race and, 35, 123
— duty of, 94
— earthly conduct concerning, 76
— enfeeblement of, in China, 170
— essentially contrived to secure material ease, if socialistic, 57
— every member of, interested in raising the general standard of living, 78
— exaltation of, under Roman Empire, 122, 132
— French, 64
— friction in a socialistic, would be caused by unselfishness and self-reliance, 41

216   THE FATE OF EMPIRES

Society (*continued*):
— has provided a link in the family that shall join the living of the present to the living of the future, 96
— hostility between the individual and the race uncovered in a rational, 52
— hostility of, to the race, 95
— identification of interests of the individual with that of, 46, 55, 57
— impoverishment of, in China, 157
— in China, 158
— in Roman Empire, 123, 128, 130, 138, 158
— individual equal to, 55
— individual incurs stress of competition in contact with, 34
— instinct the enemy of, 83
— interaction of interest of individual with that of, 33
— interest of, 33, 57, 83, 156
— interest of individual in relation to, 34, 36, 42, 45, 46, 55, 56
— interest of the race and, 34, 35, 55, 64, 98, 146, 178
— involved in horrible conditions in China, 174
— logical position of, *vis-à-vis* to the race, 58
— members of, seek their own ends under socialistic conditions, 46
— moral position of individual in a world wherein all property would be invested in, 78
— most splendid period of Roman, 138
— mutual dependence of the individual, the race, and, 94
— mutual relations of the race and, 94
— new attitude of, under method of religious motive, 95
— no more than individuals acting in concert, 94
— of unparalleled magnificence under the Roman Empire, 123
— office of, under method of religious motive, 96
— our duties to, 89
— racial duty of, 95
— racial ideas shut out from meaning attached to the word, 33
— rational character of a non-competitive, 42
— rational relations of the individual and, 55
— reaps the benefit of death duties, 98
— relations between the race and, 34, 55, 59, 94
— religious motive retains the element of liberty in, 85
— riches spent upon, under method of reason, 88
— same character in Greek and in Roman civilisation, 148
— splendour of Roman, 139
— State not ancillary to, in China, 170
— strife between a given individual and, 34, 37

INDEX 217

Society (*continued*):
— takes the place of the individual *vis-à-vis* to the race, 56, 58
— the family in its contact with, shown in cognation, 136
— the family in relation to, 97
— the necessary work of, how carried on in the absence of competition, 39
— the subjection of the individual to, under the method of religious motive, 85
— the unit of, is not the family, 99
— under a system of common ownership, 56
— under the influence of religious motive, 86, 98
— under the method of reason, 55, *et seq.*
— use of the word, 33
Soranus, 140
Spain, 171
Species:
— actual struggle for life is among the young of every, 16
— how does the individual fare as apart from? 14
— instinct leads to the most rapid reproduction of, 16
— perpetuation of, under method of instinct, 13
— stress involved in the rearing of the young of the, 17
— subordination of the individual to the interests of the, 29
— the care of the young of the, and the true interest of the adult animal, 14
Spencer (Herbert), 26, 27, 41
State:
— and patriotism count for very little in China, 170
— assumption of supreme and intrusive power in Rome, 108
— can barely exist in China, 156
— Chinaman careless of the, 167
— Chinese religion no polity of the, 156
— Church and, Augustus becomes head of both in Rome, 112
— compulsion, the curse of, 86
— convulsed for thirteen years in Rome after the death of Julius Cæsar, 111
— encouragement of geocentric religions by Roman, 116, 117
— good and evil in the, discovery of, 4
— feebleness of, as a source of disaster in China, 170
— less able members prevented from contributing to the numbers of the Greek, 150
— maintained by influx of aliens in Rome, 145
— necessity, manumission of slaves under Roman Empire was a, 145
— only exists for the sake of the family, 108, 109, 170
— religion as an instrument of, 116, 117
— religion recognised by, 116, 117

State (*continued*):
— religions that subserved the, 108, 114
— the married, aversion from, under Roman Empire, 138
— the Roman, and abolition of competition, 128, *et seq.*
— vacant legacies inherited by, under Roman Empire, 142
— weakness of, in China, 171

Steam locomotion:
— admits of little further improvement, and is already passing into a less prominent position, 8, 9
— supersedes sailing-ship and old system of coaching, 8

Stimulus:
— need of a power to act independently of, 69, 70
— of competition, 39, 41
— reflex response to, 9, 10, 63, 68, 69
— the respiratory centre called into action by, 10

Stress:
— and anxiety falling upon parents, 51
— competitive or social, 16, 30, 32, 34, 48, 50, 52, 58, 61, 72, 74, 77, 78, 86, 93, 100, 101, 158, 178
— complete cessation of the competitive, demanded by reason, 38, *et seq.*
— escape from racial, only possible by avoidance of parenthood, 58
— involved in the rearing of the young of the species, 17
— no material difference to the individual, 58
— of life, 31, 51, 72
— racial or reproductive, 32, 34, 43, 50, 54, 56–58, 61, 63, 72, 87, 93, 100–102, 109
— rational revolt against social and racial, practically simultaneous, 60, *et seq.*
— revolt against racial, under Roman Empire, 137, 139
— revolt against social, under Roman Empire, 128, *et seq.*
— still arises from the same two causes, 31
— the abolition of, under method of reason, 32, *et seq.*
— the general, of life and the method of religious motive, 72

Stresses:
— endurance of the two, under the method of religious motive, 101
— incidence of two, must be examined separately, 32
— severity of both, relieved under reason, 31
— social and racial, 60
— the revolt against, under reason, 60
— the two essential, 31, 51, 72
— two great permanent, 31, 74, 77
— which should be modified? 32

INDEX 219

Suetonius, 123
Sustenance:
— animal world brings forth its young in numbers that far exceed the limits of, 15
— animal world long ago reached the limit of, 16, 30
— to man the possible limits of, outrun reproduction, 31
Syllogism:
— man's only sword and only shield, 28
Syndicalism:
— a blend of, with Socialism under Roman Empire, 128

TACITUS, 123, 127, 143, 145
Taeping Rebellion, 171
Tao:
— is not *ad hoc*, 156
— means "The Path," 153
— rules in virtue of its own authority, 156
— the ancient core of Chinese belief, 153
— the path of Creation, 156
Taoism:
— makes no attempt to deal with competitive stress, 177
— of Confucius, 156
— takes nothing into account except the family, 169
Tertullian, 121
Thebes, 176
Theology (the domain of), 178
Thucydides, 151
Tiber, 147
Tiberianus, 120
Tiberius, 143
Titus, 118
Touchstone:
— a common factor that will furnish a, 67
Trades Unions:
— Chinese analogue of, 158
— in the Roman Empire, 128
Trajan, 120

UNIFICATION:
— of effort under method of reason, 57
United Kingdom, 171
Usus:
— a form of marriage in the Roman Empire, 137, 138

VESPASIAN, 118

WASTE:
— inevitable in the method of instinct, 17, 20, 25
— inevitable in the vegetable world, 18
— limitless under instinct, 72
— of effort, 17, 45, 46
— the avoidance of, under reason, 45
— to prevent, has been the office of reason, 46

Wastefulness:
— avoidance of instinctive, 24
— beyond our powers of conception, 17
— environment of, created by instinct, 62
— inevitable in the method of instinct, 18, 19
— limitless in the method of instinct, 38
— method of, inconceivable, 77
— of effort obviated by reason, 45
— of reason parallel to that of instinct, 63
— of the environment created by instinct, 62
— of the primitive method, 45
— practically without limit under instinct, 17

White man:
— Chinese mind incomprehensible to the, 169
— civilisation of, not yet under religious motive, 100
— does not easily realise the meaning of ancestor-worship, 153 ʼ
— every community of the, shows failure of birthrate, 53
— possesses the records of past civilisations, 3
— suffers in contest of wits with Chinaman, 167
— the average, inferior to average Chinaman, 166

Will:
— freedom of, 75, 81

Women:
— position of, assured in China, 173
— the " Higher Education " of, in America leads to avoidance of office, 53

Worship. *See* Ancestor